Digging for Ancestral Gold

The Fun and Easy Way
to Get Started
on Your Genealogy Quest

Laurence Overmire

INDELIBLE MARK PUBLISHING

Indelible Mark Publishing 2016

Editing, cover/interior design, author photos: Nancy McDonald

Front cover photo:
Sara Tarr/Shutterstock.com

Back cover map image:
toadberry/Shutterstock.com

Library of Congress Control Number 2016947873

ISBN 978-0-9795398-7-9

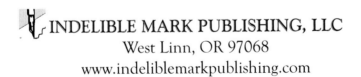
INDELIBLE MARK PUBLISHING, LLC
West Linn, OR 97068
www.indeliblemarkpublishing.com

To family researchers everywhere
who dedicate their time and energy to
restoring and preserving the memory
of those who have gone before

History remembers only the celebrated.
Genealogy remembers them all.

~ Laurence Overmire

Books by Laurence Overmire

The Ghost of Rabbie Burns
An American Poet's Journey Through Scotland

The McDonalds of Lansingburgh, Rensselaer
County, New York
The Pioneering Family of Richard and Catharine
(Lansing) McDonald and Their Descendants

William R. McDonald and Abigail Fowler of
Herkimer County, New York and Their
Descendants

A Revolutionary American Family
The McDonalds of Somerset County, New Jersey

The One Idea That Saves the World
A Call to Conscience and A Call to Action

Gone Hollywood

One Immigrant's Legacy
The Overmyer Family in America, 1751-2009

Report From X-Star 10

Honor & Remembrance
A Poetic Journey through American History

TABLE OF CONTENTS

PREFACE

When I started doing genealogy in the early 1990's, the Internet was just beginning to catch fire. I knew very little about my ancestry. Sure, I had some names and dates going back a few generations, but I had no idea of the wealth of information that would soon lie literally at my fingertips. Thanks to the Internet, people around the globe are now able to find and share their genealogical materials, and, as a result, what used to take years of diligent and painstaking research can now be accomplished in a relatively short period of time using only your personal device (laptop, PC, iPad, etc.). This book will show you how.

My remarkable journey through the branches of my own ancestral tree revealed a descent from Charlemagne, Alfred the Great, William the Conqueror, Edward III, Robert the Bruce of Scotland, Revolutionary War and Civil War veterans, three Native American lines, nine Mayflower pilgrims and hundreds of other American immigrants and pioneers. I was also amazed to find that I shared common ancestors with people like Sir Winston Churchill, Thomas Edison, Walt Disney, Robert Frost, Emily Dickinson, Katherine Hepburn, Humphrey Bogart, Henry Fonda and John Wayne, to name only a few. They were my cousins, albeit distant ones.

At first I was astonished to find that I was related to so many famous people. As I continued on my quest, however,

I discovered that there was nothing unique or special about my ancestral heritage at all. The fact is, we are all related. We are all literally cousins. Everyone has an amazing ancestral tree waiting to reveal itself – IF they can find it.

Moreover, all of us are connected to the entirety of human history. You will find that your ancestors have many different skin colors and many different religions and cultures.

The truth of our genealogy, then, is much much greater than most of us have ever taken the time to consider.

The fun lies in actually finding the connections and seeing how your family descends from the ancient historical past.

Knowing who you are and how you fit into the Big Picture is critical to your self-image and your sense of compassion for and connection to our extended human family.

Someday, because you picked up this book and decided to trace your family tree, your 7th or 8th great-grandchild will find you in the ever-widening branches of his heritage and say, "Thank you. I'm grateful for all you did to preserve our family's history. I'm honored to be your descendant."

Every human being should be immortalized in the memories of his or her descendants. By recalling your ancestors and remembering their lives, you do them honor; you grant them immortality.

I wish you great success on this the beginning of your own incredible journey through your family's long and ancient history.

Laurence Overmire
Family Historian and Genealogist
West Linn, Oregon, USA

CHAPTER 1

Why Genealogy Is So Important

There is no nobler profession, nor no greater calling, than to be among those unheralded many who gave and give their lives to the preservation of human knowledge, passed with commitment and care from one generation to the next.

That's what I tell audiences when I am asked to speak about genealogy.

You, dear reader, must be one of those rare people who knows how important this work is. You really care about family. You appreciate knowing family history and sharing it with those you love. In my book, that makes you a very special person.

You may already understand that all of humanity is one large family. All of us are, in fact, related. We are all, at the very least, distant cousins.[1] It doesn't matter where people come from, what color they are, what language they speak, what their religion or their politics, they are your cousins. But how many of us live our lives that way – in the knowledge that we are all one big family, brothers and sisters?

When you feel connected to the human family, when you know you are connected in every atom of your being, you are whole. You feel loved. You feel like you belong. Problems arise when a person feels disconnected. In extreme cases, those disaffections can produce aberrant or criminal behaviors. This is true on a societal level as well – the difficulties we see in the world right now are manifestations of our disconnection from one another.

We are living at a crucial time in history when humanity needs to come together to solve the very serious problems in the world. Working together in mutual respect, helping one another – that's how communities thrive. That's the world we all want to live in, isn't it? In order to make this come about, we will need to focus on our connection to one another, our common humanity. Genealogy is one of the tools that can take us there – to a better world for all.

---

[1] John P. Hussman Institute for Human Genomics, Miller School of Medicine, University of Miami, high.med.miami.edu, accessed June 2016; see also J. Craig Venter Institute, "Genome Variations," Genome News Network, genomenewsnetwork.org, accessed June 2016. Genetically speaking, all humans are 99.9% identical, i.e. they share 99.9% of their DNA with each other.

THE SEVENTH GENERATION PRINCIPLE

Native American traditions say that **the decisions we make today will affect the next seven generations.** Therefore, it is very important to consider how our decisions might affect those future generations. Seven generations is roughly about 175-300 years.[2] There is a lot of truth in this idea. If you know your ancestors' stories going back a few hundred years, you can actually see how their lives have had an impact on yours – physically, economically, emotionally, and spiritually. That's why the quest for your ancestral gold can be so richly rewarding.

If we really take the time to think about it, we might begin to see that the impact of our lives is even greater than we can imagine. There is a rippling effect. Every action we take, positive or negative, has consequences that spread out into the world like ripples on a pond. Most of these consequences will occur without our awareness. We can never know the true effects our lives have on others, the things we say and do, but we can rest assured, given this rippling effect, that what we do today will have an impact on humanity – and this planet, and by extension, the Universe – forevermore, to the end of time. Why? Because everything is interconnected. There is an interdependent web of existence. We all need each other and we all affect each other.

---

[2] Donn Devine, "How long is a generation? Science provides an answer," International Society of Genetic Genealogy Wiki, isogg.org, accessed June 2016.

Think of your ancestry. You have billions of ancestors going back, back, back in time. Without any one of these people, you would not be here. All of them, in that sense, are equally important.

To demonstrate this a little more clearly, imagine your descendants four hundred years from now. That would be about the year 2416 C.E. (Common Era or Current Era).[3] Do those descendants four hundred years in the future mean anything to you today as you sit here now? Do you want them to prosper, to be happy? Do you care what happens to them at all? And if not, why not? They are, after all, your flesh and blood. They are the children of your children.

Have you ever thought how many descendants you might have 400 years from now, assuming you now have children? Well, to give you an idea, four hundred years ago in the early 1600's, the first immigrants came to America. Some have estimated that each of those immigrants, if they had children who survived, now has about a million descendants or more. Think about that. If any one of those immigrants never existed, one million people today would disappear from the face of the Earth.

RICHARD WARREN AND ELIZABETH WALKER

Let's take a specific example: Richard Warren and his wife Elizabeth Walker. Richard Warren was a merchant

---

[3] C.E. is equivalent to A.D., though the former is more commonly used in recent times.

and haberdasher from London who was born in 1580. He came to America on the Mayflower in 1620.

Do you think he and his wife Elizabeth ever sat around at the dining room table and asked themselves, "Who do you think years from now our descendants might be?" Well, folks, if Richard Warren and Elizabeth Walker had never existed, the following people among their descendants would never have been born:

Presidents Franklin Delano Roosevelt and Ulysses S. Grant; poet Henry Wadsworth Longfellow; authors Henry David Thoreau and Laura Ingalls Wilder; artist Winslow Homer; inventor of the sewing machine Elias Howe; Chef Julia Child; publisher Frank Nelson Doubleday; Roger Nash Baldwin (Founder of the ACLU); Brian Wilson and his brothers known as "The Beach Boys;" the Wright Brothers; Amelia Earhart; astronaut Alan B. Shepard; Orson Welles; Tonight Show host Johnny Carson; and to top it all off, this book would disappear because this author wouldn't be here either.[4]

So you see, all of our lives would be drastically different if Richard Warren and Elizabeth Walker never existed. The same can be said of almost any individual. Hundreds of years from now, a multitude of your descendants will be beholden to you as well. And some of them, if not most of

---

[4] For the specific lineages of these people and how they descend from Richard and Elizabeth Warren, see *The Ancestry of Overmire, Tifft, Richardson, Bradford, Reed,* by Laurence Overmire (RootsWeb WorldConnect project, 2016).

them in an enlightened future age, will want to know who you were. What was your story? What can they learn from YOU and your time on this Earth.

The fact that you are reading this book, that you are considering embarking on your own quest of ancestral discovery, tells us a lot about what sort of person you are: a person who deeply cares. That's something to be proud of. And it is something your descendants will want to know about you. Believe me, as someone who is so thankful for the genealogists and family researchers who have gone before, who wishes that I could thank them personally, let me say that the work that you do in researching your family history is of vital importance to all who will come after. They will be forever grateful for your efforts.

THE REDWOOD TREE

Now at this point, I want to take you on a little imaginary journey...

Imagine, if you will, a beautiful redwood tree. Can you see it in your mind's eye? It's huge. It goes up and up and up and up and up. You can't even see the top. Now imagine that around this redwood tree is a tall fence. No matter what you do, you can't touch that tree. But you notice that there's a small twig on the ground. You can just barely reach it. Grab a hold of it and pull it out through the fence. Have you got it? Good.

Now I want you to hold up your little imaginary twig. Take a good look at it. It's only a few inches long. The redwood represents the human family tree. We are all connected in this tree. We are, all of us, family. Regardless of nationality, color, religion, whatever, we are all related! Scientists at National Geographic say our common ancient ancestors from whom we are all descended, our genetic Adam and Eve, if you will, lived in Africa about 60,000 years ago.[5]

The twig represents the portion of our family tree that we can actually identify and trace. This is as good as it gets. As a genealogist, my twig is probably several inches bigger than yours, but it's still a twig or a short stick. With over 20 years of searching, I've found about eighteen thousand of my ancestors and about a hundred thousand of their descendants and relations. That may seem like a lot, but in truth it's quite miniscule, considering how many ancestors actually comprise our tree.

The problem is that documentary evidence like civil and church records are almost non-existent prior to about 1650. So for most ordinary people, the so-called "commoners," it's very difficult to get back prior to 1650. For the nobility, on the other hand, people of great wealth and status, we can trace far back in time because records do exist, particularly records showing how land and property is passed down from generation to generation. That's why so many people today claim to be descended from royalty and not from the peasants who worked in the

---

[5] Spencer Wells, *Deep Ancestry: Inside the Genographic Project* (National Geographic, 2006).

kitchens and tilled the fields. You simply can't find the lower classes. They have disappeared from history.

Getting back to our analogy, the fence of time prevents us from getting close to that redwood tree, but we know it's there, even if we can only retrieve a small twig.

And let's also keep in mind that everyone on this Earth shares a common ancestry that stretches back about 200,000 years to the dawn of Homo sapiens (Latin: "wise person") in Africa.[6] So most of that huge redwood tree represents the countless ancestors we all have in common.

WHAT ARE THE IMPLICATIONS OF ALL THIS?

Well, for one thing it means we need to keep careful records from this time forward and hand down important family information. Isn't it a tragedy that so many of our ancestors have been lost forever? Let's not allow that to happen to our loved ones. Let's remember and honor their passage on this Earth.

Knowing your genealogy will also challenge you to open those parts of yourself that you have previously ignored, to take equal pride in those maternal branches as well as the patriarchal surname you call your own.

Most importantly, it will challenge you to become a more compassionate human being. To really see others, no matter how different, as members of your own family,

---

[6] "What does it mean to be human: Homo sapiens," Smithsonian National Museum of Natural History, 2016, humanorigins.si.edu, accessed June 2016.

to embrace the ne'er-do-wells, the scoundrels, and the people you just don't like or understand. You will find that your ancestors include peoples of different political persuasions and different colors and different religions. Remember they are your grandparents. Are you going to hate them because they had a different religion than yours? Or they spoke a different language? I don't think so; I think you will find that you will love them just as they are (or were), because they are a part of you now.

THE DISTANCE OF RELATIONSHIPS

But what about the distance of the relationships? Should we place more significance on someone who is a 4th cousin, for example, than on someone who is a half 7th cousin 3 times removed? What does the distance mean, anyway? There's a level of absurdity here that is very difficult to wrap your mind around, isn't there?

I'm going to suggest to you, that the **distance in time and space** in your relationships doesn't really matter as much as you might think, the fact that there *is* **relationship**, however, does matter.

Remember what scientists have been telling us about time itself. Einstein said that time is an illusion; that past, present and future exist simultaneously. The distance in time is an illusion as well. How can you possibly quantify or qualify the difference between a 5th great-grandfather and a 25th great-grandfather? After all, without either one, you wouldn't be here.

THE QUANTUM FIELD OF ANCESTRY

For those who are scientifically inclined, I might suggest to you that your ancestry is like a quantum field. In truth, the number of your ancestors going back in time is astronomical. They are all real. They were real people who begat your forefathers and mothers who eventually gave birth to you. But you won't know any of them – they will not be real to you – until you choose to focus on them, that is, in quantum terms, "observe" them. Once observed, they will indeed become real to you and in some mystic, indefinable way, become an integral, conscious part of who you are.

The choice is always ours to make. We may choose to think that these ancient ancestors don't matter – and if we don't seek them out, they won't matter, at least in any meaningful, conscious way. My own experience tells me that they really do matter, that is, if we allow them to matter. We can always close the door on any experience in life. You can close the door on your ancestors and they won't mean a thing to you, and you probably won't have the vaguest idea of the precious treasure you will have lost.

It's not really about the ancestors, though, is it? It's about *you*. About who *you* are. If you can make those ancestors real for yourself, learn their stories and who they were, *your* life – and death – will take on added MEANING. You will see yourself in the BIG PICTURE that includes all human life that has come and gone on the planet. People may appear to you right now as strangers in your present mindset, but you'll soon discover that they aren't really strangers at all. They're cousins whom you just haven't met yet!

Take a few moments and let that sink in.

In the next chapter we'll take a look at how easy it is to get started on your quest.

NOTES

NOTES

CHAPTER 2

Preparing for Your Ancestral Quest

Did you ever have the experience as a young boy or girl of going on a hunt for buried treasure? Or perhaps you saw one of those old pirate movies where they went searching for the long-lost stash of gold doubloons and pieces of eight.

Or maybe you've always had a penchant for archaeology, for digging through the layers of earth in search of age-old civilizations.

Or you might be one of those folks who loves a good mystery. Have you ever wanted to be the detective that finds all the clues and solves the crime?

Well, now's your chance. Going on the hunt for your ancestors and looking for important clues that lead to their discovery is no less suspenseful and exciting! A lot of people say it's more entertaining than doing a crossword puzzle or watching TV – and infinitely more meaningful.

This is a journey that promises to be a lot of fun! No doubt you will recapture that childlike sense of adventure as you begin to unravel the mystery of your ancient forebears. The riches you uncover may not have any monetary value, but their spiritual value is priceless. When you find a piece of gold from your ancestral past, it's like winning the lottery! Each nugget will have some effect on your personal identity – who you think you are and where you come from. What you learn can be handed down to your children and their children after them. The family tree that you discover, once recorded, will be a lasting legacy for your family in times to come.

WHAT YOU WILL NEED

Thankfully, you won't need a bucket and a shovel on this dig for ancestral gold. You won't even have to get your pants dirty. All you will need to get started is a PC, Mac, laptop or handheld device, an Internet connection, any good family tree software, and a few simple facts.

GENEALOGY SOFTWARE

There are a number of good family tree software programs on the market. Two popular ones are Family Tree Maker and Legacy. Reunion is a good one for those with Macs. Basically, you are looking for a user-friendly, affordable program. I don't work for any of these companies, so I don't recommend one over another, but I do suggest you research them before purchasing to find the one that suits you. Most are comparable and have similar features and capabilities.

Once you've selected your software program, spend some time familiarizing yourself with how it works. You will see that there are individual records that you will create for each person that can be assembled into family records that include all the members of an immediate family.

Each individual record has a field for you to enter birth, death, burial, and marriage(s). These are the essential pieces of information including dates and places, if known. Beyond that you can add additional information, such as baptism, occupation, education, religion, etc. With each set of parents, you can attach records for their children and spouses.

Here's an example from Reunion's software program:

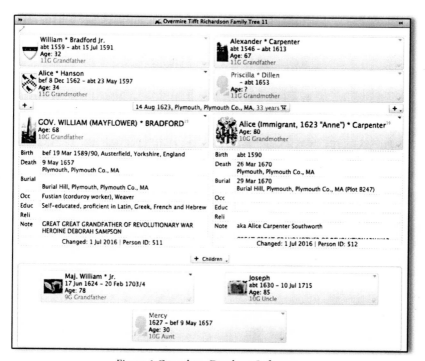

Figure 1 Genealogy Database Software

One of the author's databases, showing a family group in Reunion 11 for Mac

Most software programs will also allow you to add digitized photos and important documents and to create charts and graphs.

Treasure Tip

If you don't have a software program, I strongly urge you to get one. It will make your genealogical research so much easier. The old pen and paper method of gathering and storing information is much too cumbersome, problematic and difficult to manage when you are trying to sort out various individuals and families. I would employ it only as a last resort.

Okay. Now that you have all your tools assembled – your computer device and software program – you are ready to get started on your adventure. You just need one more thing: a map to guide you on our quest!

THE ANCESTRAL TREASURE MAP

Every good quest needs a treasure map. So take a few minutes to create yours.

Let's find out how much you already know about your immediate ancestors. On page 20, you will find an Ancestral Treasure Map. Take a few minutes to write down the last names, or surnames, of your father, your mother, grandparents, etc. If you remember them all, you'll have 8 surnames for your great-grandparents. These

8 names represent what I call your "primary heritage." They are primary because they have the most immediate impact upon you both genetically and spiritually.

If you have any blanks among your primary ancestors, people and surnames whom you have not identified, that is a good place to begin your quest.

 Treasure Tip

As a genealogist you will always be looking for answers to solve the mysteries. With each question that you solve, many more questions will arise. Allow your curiosity to guide you. What would you like to find out more about? Is it the history of the time? The place? The person's occupation? Where they went to church or school? Follow your passions. In this sense, genealogy can be a great educational tool. You will learn so much about life. Genealogy should never be boring!

Ancestral Treasure Map

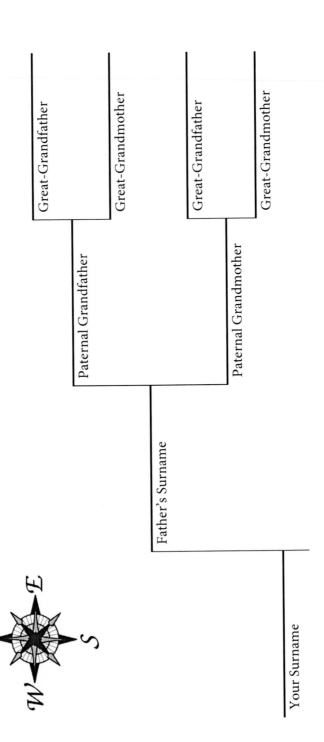

Great-Grandfather

Great-Grandmother

Paternal Grandfather

Great-Grandfather

Great-Grandmother

Paternal Grandmother

Father's Surname

Your Surname

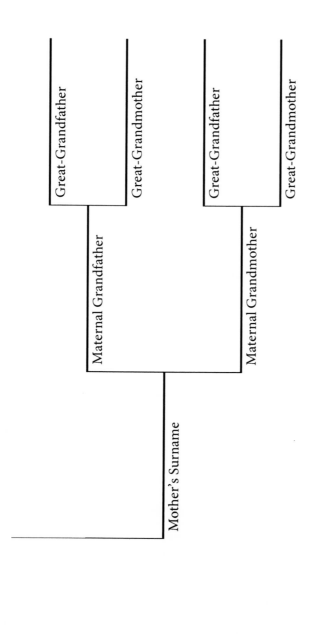

Enter all the surnames (last names) you know in the chart above.

SURNAMES

Let's take a look at the surnames on your Ancestral Treasure Map. These names will reveal important clues about your ancestral heritage. As you can see from the chart below, surnames didn't come into widespread use until about 1450 C.E. or so. The spellings of surnames in many cases were not fixed until the 20th century. It is not unusual for different people from the same family lineage to spell their surname in several different ways. In my own family, the German surname Obermeyer was also spelled Obermayer, Obermeier, Obermoyer, Obermair and Obermier and was later anglicized to Overmire, Overmier, Overmyer, Overmeyer and Overmoyer.

SURNAME ORIGINS

- ➢ 2800 B.C.E. – surnames first used, in China.
- ➢ Surnames were used during some periods in Rome. As the Roman Empire declined, however, single names were once again in vogue.
- ➢ 900 C.E. – hereditary surnames appear in Italy.
- ➢ The Crusades spread surnames throughout Europe, initially to nobility and landowners.
- ➢ By 1100 C.E. – surnames common, especially among nobility.
- ➢ By 1450, most people of whatever rank or class had a fixed hereditary surname.
- ➢ The spelling of many surnames was not fixed until the 20th century.

There are four main categories of surname derivation.

1. **Localities or Places.** These surnames were often associated with the wealthy who possessed Baronies, Manors or Fiefs. Examples: Hamilton (Manor of Hambledon, meaning fortified mansion), Murray (County of Moray, Scotland, meaning Great Water), Pratt (from Latin meaning meadow), Waite (meadow), Weston (west town), Burns (a burn is a stream), Woods, Rivers, Stone.

2. **Nicknames describing the person.** Examples: Lyons (Gaelic, grey); Boyd (Gaelic, yellow-haired), Gammons (meaning leg, something related to leg or gait), Merriman (merry man).

3. **Occupation or social status.** Examples: Baker, Bishop, Potter, Smith, Foster (forester), Bailey (from bailiff), Parsons (clergy), Schreiber (German, writer).

4. **Patronymic.** These surnames derive from the first name of the father or grandfather. Examples: Johnson, Pearson (Pierre's son or son of Peter), Hopkins (meaning little Robert or son of Robert), McDonald (son of Donald), Hansson (Swedish, son of Hans).

To find out the meaning and origin of any particular surname, just do a quick search on the Internet (name + surname + meaning) and you will usually find some pertinent information.

Take a moment to think about your own surname. For most people, their surname came from their father – handed down generation by generation from father to son back to about 1450 or before. I'd like you to consider a few questions. To what extent is your identity shaped by this name? Do you feel more of a kinship with someone who has the same male surname than with someone who has a name you share from a female line? Which brings up the issue, just how sexist are we? How much has our very identity been shaped by a patriarchal society?

Now take a look at your treasure map again. Ask yourself how far back in time you can go on each of those surnames. For example, I can go back to 1660 on my father's Overmire line, but only 1810 on my mother's Mitchelson line. My paternal grandmother Tifft's line goes all the way back to Charlemagne.

Can you trace any of your lines before the 1800's?

Now ask yourself, at this point in time, before you've really started to do some digging, who do you expect your ancestors will be? Will they be from a certain social class? Would they share a common ethnicity or religious persuasion? Might they come from a specific foreign country or continent?

In your current idea of yourself as you read this book, do you think you are descended from ordinary people, the so-called "commoners," or are you descended from aristocracy, even royalty? Do you think, by any chance, you are related to famous people? Who might they be?

Whatever your preconceptions are, be forewarned. The truth about your ancestry may blow your mind.

Brace yourself for the next chapter…

NOTES

NOTES

CHAPTER 3

Blowing Your Mind

I want to warn you that this treasure hunt, like any worthwhile quest, involves a certain amount of risk and danger. What you discover may completely change your idea of who you thought you were. You may uncover things that you were led to believe were true, but are, in fact, false.

More often than not, however, what you discover about your family roots will blow your mind in a good way.

So put your seat belts on and hang on to your hats. What I'm about to say has the potential to alter our consciousness, and if we grasp its implications, may even be a force for change in the world.

From my work as a genealogist having studied the trees of thousands of people, I can say with complete confidence that, although you may not be aware of it, you are descended from royalty. No matter what your nationality, you are descended from the ancient kings and queens or tribal leaders of your particular continent of origin, be it Europe, Asia, Africa, Australia or the Americas.[7]

Moreover, through the various branches of your tree, you are connected to the entirety of human history. When we talk about the ancient Egyptians building the pyramids, we're not talking about a bunch of exotic strangers, we're talking about our great- great- many times great-grandparents!

HOW CAN THIS BE TRUE?

It's all in the numbers. Let's take a look at the following chart.

With every generation, the number of your grandparents doubles. Starting with yourself as the first generation, you have four grandparents. Then at generation 2, you have 8 great-grandparents – four on your father's side and four on your mother's side. These are the primary ancestors we talked about before.

Generation 3 has 16 great-great-grandparents; generation 4 has 32 great-great-great-grandparents, and so on.

Gov. William Bradford is my 10th great-grandfather. He came to America on the Mayflower in 1620. I should explain that this chart is relative to me. I was born in 1957. Bradford and other Mayflower Pilgrims are at my 13th generation (starting with myself as the 1st generation), meaning that, at that level, I have 16,384 grandparents.

---

[7] Those royal ancestors may be far, far back in time, but they are there nonetheless.

BY THE NUMBERS

Generation	# Grandparents	Approximate Time*	World Population**
1	4	Current (2016)	7+ Billion
2	8	World War II (1939-1945)	2.5 Billion
3	16	World War I (1914-1918)	1.8 Billion
4	32	1890	1.5 Billion
5	64	American Civil War (1861-1865)	1.3 Billion
9	1,024	American Revolution (late 18th Century)	820 Million
13	16,384	Gov. Wm. Bradford (Mayflower, 1620)	560 Million
17	262,144	16th Century (Henry VIII)	500 Million
22	8,388,608	14th Century (Edward III)	439 Million
24	33,544,432	13th Century (Edward I)	430 Million
30	2.1 Billion	1066 (William the Conqueror)	360 Million
36	137.4 Billion	Charlemagne (c.742-814)	300 Million
52	9 Quadrillion	3rd Century CE	260 Million

*Note that the approximate times shown are relative to the author's family tree.

**Scott Manning, "Year-by-Year World Population Estimates: 10,000 B.C. to 2007 A.D.," Appendix: World Population Estimate Sets, Jan 12, 2008, scottmanning.com, accessed June 2016.

Figure 2 Number of Grandparents Related to World Population

The numbers will be different if you are a generation or two younger or older than me. If you're a generation older, Gov. Bradford and the Mayflower Pilgrims will be your twelfth generation and the number of your grandparents will be half of my number or about 8,192. If you are a generation younger, this will be your 14th generation and you will have 33,668 grandparents at this Mayflower level.

Jumping to the 22nd generation, the level of the English king, Edward III, in my chart, we have over 8 million grandparents.

William the Conqueror, who became the first Norman king of England following the Battle of Hastings in 1066 C.E., is at my 30th generation with over 2.1 billion grandparents at that level. Yes, that's "B" as in BILLION. Did you ever think you might be a descendant of William the Conqueror? Well, if you have English ancestry, then there's a very good chance he was one of those billions of your grandparent ancestors. Remember, too, that most of those ancestors were probably peasants who didn't even have surnames. No records remain to help us in finding them. They are forever lost. Also consider that there were only about 360 million people on the planet at that time.

Charlemagne (c. 742-814 C.E.) is at my 36th generation and is just one of roughly 137 billion grandparents at that level. Yet the entire world population at the time was only about 300 million. You might be asking, how can you have more grandparents than there were people on the planet?

The reason is that not all of those grandparents are different individuals. In times past people not infrequently married their 2nd, 3rd, 4th, 5th cousins, etc., so they were descended from the same grandparents back in time. If you look at Charlemagne, for example, you will find that you don't descend from just one of his children, you descend from several of his many children. These children obviously share the same grandparents.

In relation to my own ancestry, the number of my grandparents begins to exceed the world population between the 27th and 28th generations, around 1100-1200 C.E. when Henry II and Eleanor of Aquitaine ruled England. From that point on, it is very clear that the actual number of your ancestors begins to decrease the further you go back in time – what genealogists call "pedigree collapse."[8]

Now if you consider the 52nd generation, somewhere around the third century C.E., you have over 9 quadrillion grandparents, yet there were only about 260 million people living on the planet at the time. In fact, it is estimated that the total number of humans who have ever lived – for all time – is only about 106-108 billion.[9] Therefore, while the number of grandparents becomes unfathomable over time, the number of our actual individual ancestors from whom we descend is in the billions.

---

[8] "Pedigree Collapse," International Society of Genealogy Wiki, isogg.org, accessed June 2016.
[9] Clara Curtin, "Fact or Fiction?: Living People Outnumber the Dead," *Scientific American* (Scientific American Inc., Mar 1, 2007), scientificamerican.com, accessed June 2016.

THE DIAMOND IN YOUR TREASURE CHEST

So you see, your actual ancestry begins to resemble a diamond as you go back in time and the world population shrinks.

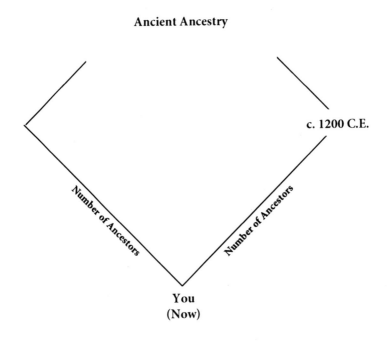

Figure 3 Pedigree Collapse

The number of your separate individual ancestors increases with each generation until you get to about the year 1200 C.E. Then, your number of ancestors becomes fewer generation by generation as the world population numbers decline.

WHEN DID OUR COMMON ANCESTORS LIVE?

Clearly, the numbers strongly suggest that the majority of us must share some common ancestry at some point not all that far back in time.

A 2004 study by professor Joseph T. Chang of Yale University, et al., using mathematical models and taking into account migration and marriage patterns, determined that we all have a common ancestor who lived as early as about 1000 B.C.E.[10] By common ancestor, we mean an individual from whom every living person on the planet is descended. (So yes, the builders of the pyramids of Egypt were likely among our common ancestors.)

Bear in mind that there may be populations living in very remote areas that may not have interacted with other genetic groups.[11] For these people, you would have to go way, way back in time to find a common ancestor with everyone else. So if the 1000 B.C.E. date postulated by Professor Chang's study is accurate, that's really not very far back in time.

Consider, also, that as soon as someone in your tree marries someone from a completely different culture, then your tree expands geographically to include all those

---

[10] Douglas L. T. Rohde, Steve Olson & Joseph T. Chang, "Modelling the recent common ancestry of all living humans," *Nature* 431, Sept 30, 2004, 562-566.

[11] As time goes on, these isolated genetic groups are becoming more and more rare as people all over the world intermingle and intermarry.

ancestors in the distant roots of that culture. For example, if you descend from Edward III of England, then you also descend from his mother, Isabella Capet, who was the daughter of the king of France, and you descend from Edward's grandmother, Eleanor of Castile, daughter of Ferdinand III, King of Leon and Castile, Spain. Through those female lines, then, you are connected to a whole host of ancestors in France and Spain.

Think of this another way: every single ancestor in your tree has his or her own huge astronomical tree filled with branches and branches of ancestors. The scope of our ancestry is really hard to wrap your mind around, isn't it?

For most of us, we share common ancestors much, much later than 1000 B.C.E. Given the enormous numbers of our ancestral grandparents, many genealogists believe that nearly everyone in Western civilization is a descendant of Charlemagne (c. 742-814 C.E.), the Father of Kings, from whom virtually the entire European monarchy descends.[12]

In my own research, which has focused primarily on Americans with immigrant ancestors from Britain who settled here in the 1600's, it is evident that many Americans living today now share common ancestry about the time of Edward III (1312-1377) or Edward I

---

[12] Landed nobility from Charlemagne on down to the present day can be traced fairly reliably with paper trails. Tracing genealogy before the time of Charlemagne, however, is typically based more on mythology than any reliable documented evidence, e.g., Norse or biblical origin stories.

(1239-1307). Not only are these people descended from those English kings (who are themselves descended from William the Conqueror and Charlemagne), but also not uncommonly from Robert the Bruce (1274-1329) of Scotland and Brian Boru (c. 941-1014) of Ireland, as well as Louis IX "St. Louis" (1214-1270) King of France.

If you have British ancestry, you too might very well be a descendant of these ancient kings. After all, when William the Conqueror of Normandy took over England beginning in 1066, his Norman knights and political favorites were granted power, subject to the king, over most of the land in the realm. The Normans infiltrated Scotland, Ireland and Wales, as well. The descendants of these Norman nobles intermarried with other ethnic groups – Angles, Saxons, Celts, Norse – so that today anyone in the British Isles who can trace at least one of their billions of ancestors into the nobility of "Olde England" would likely find themselves descending from William the Conqueror and the early Plantagenet kings.

THE MYTH OF ROYAL BLOOD

Having royal blood in the Middle Ages may have commanded some preferential significance and may have set the nobility apart from the rest of impoverished, struggling humanity, but nowadays that mythical blood has been handed down after so many generations to the rest of us. We all descend from the ancient kings and tribal chieftains of our various ethnic cultures. We are all truly equal in that respect.

But before we get too full of ourselves and start boasting about our royal heritage, let's take a reality check: most of those ancient kings and wealthy nobles were pretty self-centered, ruthless people who lived in depressingly barbarous times. An honest, poor, but otherwise unremarkable man and his loving, tender-hearted wife, though long forgotten and lost to history, may have been the ancestors who are most worthy of our admiration today.

The more you dig into history, into the truth about human beings, the more you discover that everyone has their flaws. After they pass away, we mythologize them and focus on their positive attributes, emphasizing and exaggerating their better qualities. But we all know, nobody's perfect.

No matter who our ancestors are, our own personal and monumental task is to become the best person that we can possibly be – someone in whom our own descendants in times to come can take great pride and find inspiration.

FAMOUS ANCESTORS AND COUSINS

Do you think you are related to famous people? Of course, you are. Everyone is. One of the fascinating things about tracing your ancestry is discovering HOW you are related to notable historical figures.

You'd think that important information, like being related to prominent people, would be handed down in the family, wouldn't you? You'd think you'd know, for example, if you were descended from someone on the

Mayflower. You'd know if one of your ancestors fought in the American Revolution. You'd know if you were descended from kings. Wouldn't that information be passed down to you? More often than not, the answer is simply NO. People were so consumed with the stresses of everyday living and dying that they simply didn't take the time, have the energy, or think it very important, to write down family history. A lot of people living today don't even know who their great-grandparents were.

The truth is that your heritage is far more rich and complex than you have ever dreamed.

Your ancestors are out there waiting to be discovered. They've been there all along. They have much to offer: wisdom, guidance, and support.

Now that we have assembled our tools – our computer device, our software program and our Treasure Map – we're ready to start our dig. What amazing things are we about to find?

NOTES

NOTES

CHAPTER 4

Gathering and Entering Data

Before logging on to the Internet to do some serious digging, gather everything you know about your ancestry to date – the names of your parents and grandparents and the dates and places of birth, death, and marriage. If you don't have this information readily available, and many people don't, no need to worry. If you have living relatives who can answer the questions, give them a call. Don't be shy. Look for letters, diaries, family bibles anything that might give you some clues.

Remember, in genealogy, TIME AND PLACE is critical. We need to know when and where people lived. It also helps to know each individual that comprises the family group, that is, the parents, the children and their spouses, if any.

Once you've gathered your information, it's time to enter everything you know with reasonable certainty into your software program. Follow the software directions about how to do so and input the data accordingly: name, date and place of birth, date and place of death, burial location, marriage date, etc. Having your information readily available to you in a software program is infinitely more expedient than doing genealogy the old-fashioned way with pen and paper. For example, a good program will easily identify your relationships from one individual in your tree to another. My program tells me that my wife is my 13th cousin once removed! I would never be able to figure that out on my own. (You think you aren't related to your spouse? Oh yes, you are! We're all literally cousins. The question is will you be lucky enough to find a connection?)

As you are entering your data, you might find that some doubts about the accuracy of the data begin to seep in. "Did my cousin Fred really know the birthplace of our great-grandfather as he wrote it down or was he just guessing?" If you aren't sure that a certain piece of information is accurate, enter it for the time being, making a note that it may be incorrect.

MAKING NOTES

Adding notes is extremely important when pursuing your ancestry. Your genealogy software program will provide you with a large field on each individual's record in which to make notes. This is where you can add all of your relevant research information for each individual including the following:

1. Birth records
2. Marriage records
3. Census records
4. Death records
5. Social Security records
6. Obituaries

7. Church records
8. Cemetery records
9. Wills
10. Military records
11. Discrepancies in the facts, e.g., different birth dates in different sources
12. Biographies
13. Local histories
14. News articles
15. Quotes from books and other sources about the individual in question
16. Correspondence with others about the individual
17. Additional sources that you'd like to check out in more detail later
18. Miscellaneous notes of any kind including any thoughts or theories you or others might have about the individual or the family group

In my software program, there are several fields for notes – miscellaneous notes, medical, military and research notes.

ADDITIONAL RECORD KEEPING

Most of your additional files can be stored on your computer. I recommend creating a folder for Genealogy. Sort records into various subfolders by surname to be able to locate them easily. Within those, you can add photographs, documents and other pertinent genealogical records.

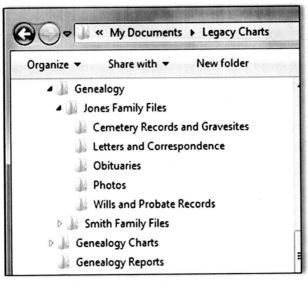

Figure 4 Example File Organization

PAPER FILES

No doubt you will also have paper files of important records and photos. You can store these in folders in a file cabinet, for example. Be sure to store them in a place where you can get to them quickly if needed. There's nothing worse than tearing your hair out trying to remember where you stored something! Believe me, I know!

BEWARE OF ERRORS

As you are assembling your data and entering it into your program, no doubt you will come across numerous inconsistencies and discrepancies among various records. That's the nature of genealogy. There is the possibility for error in every step of the record-making process. Inaccuracies abound. Especially on the Internet.

As we've all learned by now, just because you find something on the Internet, doesn't mean it's true. This is particularly the case when it comes to genealogy. Consider the information that you find to be a clue, not a fact, unless you can verify a credible source of the information. As you are researching, it is very important to **note the source** of each piece of information that you enter in your database.

The next chapter will show you how.

NOTES

NOTES

CHAPTER 5

Sourcing, Plagiarism, and Copyright Law

Sourcing is essential to genealogy.

HOW TO SOURCE

As you collect and enter data, note the source in your database. Include the title of the work, the author, the publisher, and the place and date of publication. Page numbers, repositories, and links to websites where applicable are helpful as well.

Here are a few example source citations just to give you an idea. Consult your software instructions for the specific procedures on how to enter sources into the program.

SOURCE CITATIONS

Book:

Laurence Overmire, *One Immigrant's Legacy: The Overmyer Family in America 1751-2009* (Indelible Mark Publishing, West Linn, OR, 2009), 125.

Newspaper:

Obituary of John Doe, *Dayton Daily News,* Dayton, OH, Feb 23, 2008, 35.

Ancestry.com:
Bill Jones, Jones Family Tree, ancestry.com,
accessed May 2016.

Census:
1940 federal census, Cleveland, Cuyahoga, OH.

Website:
"Jacobite Rebellion Ships," Immigrant Ships
Transcribers Guild, immigrantships.net, accessed
Aug 2016.

As you can see, it is important to note the date a
website was accessed. This is due to the changing nature of
websites, which are updated frequently.

WHY SOURCE?

In essence, the issue is this: anyone reading your
genealogy research needs to know where you got your
information, particularly so if you publish your
information for public consumption.

Why? Because genealogy is fraught with error. It's the
nature of the beast. There is the possibility for human
error in every step of the record-making as well as the
record-keeping process. People make mistakes all the
time.

AVOIDING FALSE INFORMATION

Just because you find something on the Internet or
even in a book doesn't mean it's true. A lot of amateur

researchers make the mistake of jumping to conclusions simply because they want to believe something is true. They publish their assumptions based on inaccurate or inadequate documentation without clarifying that what they are posting is speculative and may not in fact be true.

These errors and myths can be handed down generation after generation and no one is the wiser. That is, until some meticulously thorough researcher takes the time to sort it all out and find the TRUTH.

Let me give you an example. When I was researching my Overmire line, there was a genealogy book published in 1905 by some very conscientious gentlemen who had taken it upon themselves to set down the Overmire family history. They gathered all the information they could on all the descendants of our immigrant ancestor, Revolutionary War Capt. John George Overmire. The book was the only real documentation of our family and was considered authoritative. Indeed, their work was critical in preserving our heritage. Unfortunately, these men were not professional genealogists, so they were not specific about where they got each piece of information. They did not include sources. They just collected bits and pieces of knowledge and put it all in a book. Apparently, someone had told them that the immigrant Captain Overmire's son George Jr. had another son named George who died in childhood. This seemingly unimportant bit of information would cause havoc and virtually disinherit thousands of Overmire descendants, who couldn't find their lineage for many, many years. As it turns out, after diligent years of research digging through land, marriage and church records, some determined descendants discovered that George, the son of George Jr., did die young, but NOT in childhood. In fact, he married and had five children, one of whom was my 3rd great-grandfather.

The lesson for all genealogical researchers is that we must be very careful about what information we put out there and provide sources as much as possible so that the data can be checked and verified by others.

 Treasure Tip

BEWARE: All sources are subject to error! Furthermore, absolute proof is very hard to come by in genealogy. Think about it; as you go back in time, there is always the possibility, albeit remote, that an individual could have been born to a different father or mother than what was commonly believed. We all know about family secrets! Even DNA evidence has its shortcomings. The findings of any genealogist, therefore, are always subject to error as well. We analyze what we believe to be the best available evidence from the most reliable sources and make our judgments accordingly.

Genealogy requires fact and evidence to assert that something is true. A good rule of thumb is to "prove" a relationship "beyond a reasonable doubt." Whenever there is nagging doubt that a person could be related to someone else, it's a sign that you need to do more research and find more evidence.

Sometimes that evidence is extremely difficult to come by, especially as you move further and further back in time. Reliable records before 1800, for example, can be quite rare.

In my own databases online, I flag an individual's record with three exclamation points (!!!) to alert them to the fact that there is a significant problem with the genealogical evidence. The lineage from child to parent or vice versa may be in serious doubt or otherwise in need of further documentation or research.

ISAAC (MAYFLOWER) * !!! ALLERTON[19]
Age: 72
10G Grandfather

Birth	abt 1586
Death	bet 1 – 12 Feb 1658/59, New Haven, New Haven Co.,
Burial	
Occ	Tailor, Assistant Governor of Plymouth, Merchant
Educ	
Reli	

Figure 5 Alert !!! in Name Field

WHAT IS A RELIABLE SOURCE?

Whenever we come across information pertaining to an individual we are investigating, we have to ask ourselves if the source is reliable and credible. Unfortunately, that is not always easy to determine.

Primary sources, that is original documents or objects of the time period in question, are usually the best sources. They could be government vital records (birth and death certificates, marriage licenses, etc.), church records of marriages and baptisms, burial and cemetery records, estate records showing purchases, sales and transfers of land, wills, probate records or other official documents of the time. But remember, even primary sources can contain errors. People can make mistakes in recording the data.

Secondary sources, that is accounts or recollections by people with no firsthand experience who were not present at the time in question, are more uncertain, but can be very helpful.

Family bibles are generally considered to be quite accurate if the dates recorded in them were made by family members who witnessed the births, the deaths and the marriages.

Family Traditions, on the other hand, must always be taken with a grain of salt. Family Traditions are those oral histories that have been handed down generation to generation. Anyone who has played "the telephone game" as a child knows how easy it is for information to get mangled or exaggerated as it passes from one storyteller to another. It is best to approach these Family Traditions as providing important clues to family history, rather than considering them to be fully accurate accounts. They usually do contain kernels of truth that are definitely worth investigating, but unless the details can be corroborated by facts and evidence, they cannot be considered completely reliable.

Newspaper and magazine articles and books are generally considered fairly reliable depending on when they were written in relation to the events in question. A Death Notice in a newspaper recorded shortly after a person's death is usually reliable in most respects, whereas a book by an author written 100 years after the event with little or no source documentation has to be approached with a healthy degree of skepticism. Keep in mind that newspaper and magazine articles can be notorious for misconstruing information and making mistakes. Anyone who has given an interview and then reads the resulting story upon publication knows this to be true. Most authors of books, on the other hand, usually have expended a good deal of time and effort in assembling their information for publication and their findings can carry more weight.

Obituaries are usually fairly accurate. Typically, family members provide the information and have their facts straight. Sometimes, however, obituaries can be misleading and faulty in their details, so beware.

Gravestones are usually accurate. They can often verify the exact dates of birth and death. But even gravestones can be misleading. I recently came across a gravestone in which the death date on the stone was shown to be inaccurate when compared to the obituary and probate records. Also watch out for gravestones that have been replaced by later generations. These stones usually look much newer than they should look. The descendants who order these new stones sometimes provide inaccurate dates to the stonecutters, because the true dates were unknown to them.

Genealogists bring years of experience and a breadth of knowledge to their interpretative work in sorting out and weighing the evidence from a variety of sources with conflicting information. Books, for example, over time develop reputations among researchers and genealogists for being trustworthy or not. If you find yourself at a loss in evaluating a source's credibility, consult a professional genealogist or experienced family researcher.

Solving the mysteries you encounter oftentimes involves applying common sense. You might, for example, have two fairly reliable sources that show different birthdates for an individual. Let's call him Joe. Source A shows Joe was born 1823 and source B shows 1828. If Joe's mother died in 1825, which birth date is more likely to be accurate? That's right – 1823! But then again, maybe an error was made in recording the death date of Joe's mother. Sound maddening? This is called "Fun with Genealogy!"

BECOMING COMFORTABLE WITH THE MYSTERY

Let's face it. Life in many ways will always be a mystery. Genealogy is much the same. It is impossible to know the truth about many things in the ancient past. Even simple things like the exact dates of a person's birth and death can be elusive.

It is impossible to know much of the truth about who our ancestors really were. How did they spend their time from day to day? What sort of personalities did they have? Were they kind? Were they generous? Were they loving and supportive parents? Did they have their own particular flaws and quirks? Would we like them if we met them? Many of these questions will always remain a mystery. All we really have are glimpses and gleanings of understanding of the people and places of times past. Let's allow that to be okay. That's life. But what we do have, what we do know, is incredibly interesting and may help to guide us as we make our way on our own life's journey.

Treasure Tip

BASIC RULE OF THUMB: Always have an open mind. Go where the evidence leads, and if new evidence presents itself, weigh it carefully, before you dare dismiss it. Remember, any source may be shown to be inaccurate as new evidence becomes available over time. Genealogy, therefore, is in a constant state of flux and requires periodic updating.

RECOMMENDATION: As you compile your data, it is important to note the discrepancies you find in various sources, especially if you cannot ascertain which pieces of information are indeed true. For example, you might find a gravestone that says a person was born in 1825 and an obituary that says he was born in 1826. In this case, it is impossible to know which is true without further research. I note these discrepancies in my own work as WARNINGS.

These WARNINGS identify discrepancies and provide information to help other researchers as they do their own investigations.

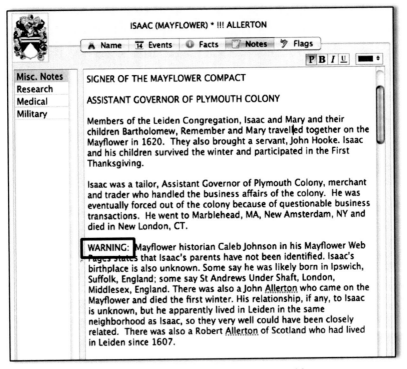

Figure 6 Place a Warning in the Note Field

PLAGIARISM AND COPYRIGHT LAW

Unfortunately, there are many unscrupulous people out there, or those who just don't know any better, who are deliberately taking the work of others, copying and pasting it into their own websites, and presenting it as their own work without giving proper credit. This is especially true on various sites all over the Internet. Others mistakenly believe that they have the right to copy and paste at will from RootsWeb, Ancestry.com, or other Internet sources, believing it is somehow in the public domain. Not so. This is plagiarism and is against the law.

It is true that anyone can use names, dates, and places – those are in the public domain, as are historical facts, but the expression of those facts is protected by copyright law. For example, if a researcher has written sentences or paragraphs about an individual (see Figure 6), that written material is his or her personal expression of the facts and evidence and must be quoted and credited if you decide to use them yourself. You may even have to get permission from the author. It is very important, therefore, for all researchers to be aware of the law. If you have any confusion about copyright law, be sure to research it on the Internet.

Regardless of the law, human decency and common courtesy demands that you credit your sources. People spend years and years in researching the material. The least we can do is to give them credit for their hard work when using their information.

REMEMBER: Whenever you quote someone else's research, cite the source. Here's an example of a properly credited online posting:

"Maj. William Bradford succeeded Myles Standish as the chief military man in the colony. He was the commander of the Plymouth forces in King Philip's War. He was wounded in battle at Narragansett Fort and carried the musket ball in his flesh the rest of his life. He also served as Assistant Treasurer and Deputy Governor of Plymouth, residing in what is now Kingston on the south side of Jones River in the same house his father lived in from 1627-47."

~ Laurence Overmire, *The Ancestry of Overmire, Tifft, Richardson, Bradford, Reed*, RootsWeb WorldConnect Project, 2016

It is also a good idea if you are quoting from an online source to provide a link to that source.

SUMMARY

> ➢ For effective genealogical work, we must provide sources. That way anyone is free to check out those sources and evaluate the material for themselves.

> ➢ It must be clear to anyone who looks at your genealogy, who wrote what. If they see that no one is quoted or sourced they will assume YOU are the source and author. If you take someone else's written expression and present it as your own, that's plagiarism and against the law.

> ➢ Websites that don't show sources have little credibility for genealogical purposes. Often they contain misleading and false information.

➢ Whenever possible, each source should include the title of the work, the author, the publisher, and the place and date of publication. Page numbers and repositories are helpful as well. If the source is a website, a link should be provided.

➢ If you cannot prove an individual's parentage beyond a reasonable doubt, keep researching for evidence and be sure to make a note of the problematic issues to anyone who consults your work.

NOTES

NOTES

CHAPTER 6

Finding Your Ancestors

Look at your treasure map again. You've input your initial data into your program and noted your sources. Now you're ready to search for more about your family history using the power of the Internet.

Identify that person on your map about whom you would like to learn more. Let's start digging and see if we can find that mysterious individual and his or her family!

First, I think we can all agree that it is a good idea to see what's out there without having to spend any money. And believe me, you can conduct a great deal of research without spending a dime.

THE 6-STEP PLAN

Every good treasure map shows a number of paces or steps that will lead you to the X that marks the spot of the buried treasure: "go 10 paces north, 5 paces northeast, and 8 paces due south until you come to the old, gnarled tree..."

By taking the following 6 steps, you will be well on your way to finding your own buried treasure.

STEP ONE: Go to RootsWeb.com

1. Access the Internet.

2. Type in the URL rootsweb.com, which takes
    you to the RootsWeb homepage.

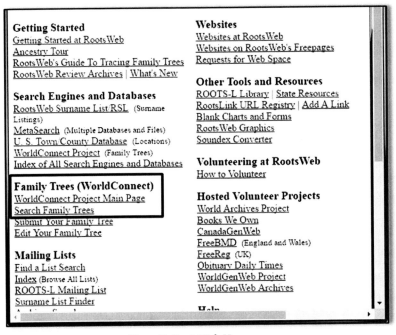

Figure 7 RootsWeb Homepage

3. Under the heading "Family Trees
    (WorldConnect)," click on the link "Search
    Family Trees." This takes you to the search
    engine, where you can enter known data about
    any ancestor and find out what information is
    available on RootsWeb, one of the best free
    Internet resources.

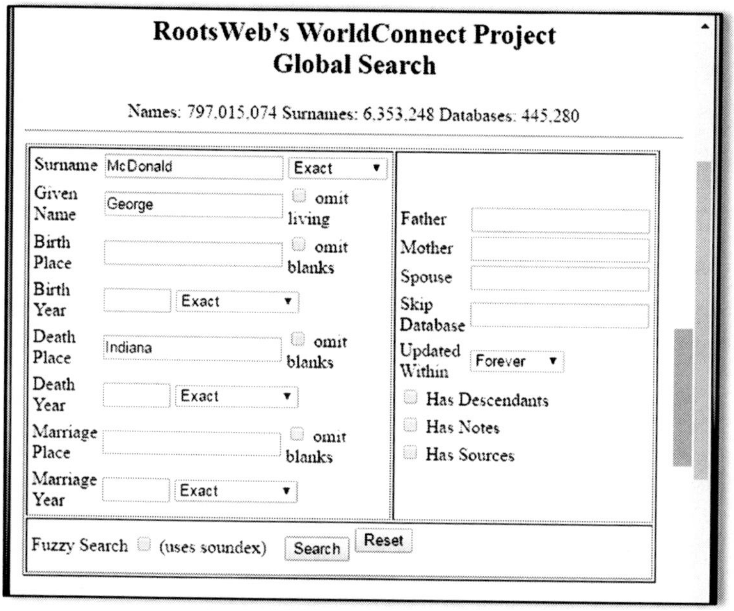

Figure 8 RootsWeb Search Screen

This is a good place to start your Internet dig. The RootsWeb site contains over 797 million names researched by people just like you from all over the world. Remember, as with any Internet site there can be inaccurate information here as well, so look for those databases that show reliable sources and quoted materials.

To search for any individual, enter their Surname (last name) and Given Name (first name). Click search and see what comes up. If there are a lot of entries that come up, then you will probably want to narrow your search by adding birth or death dates or places. You might also add parents or spouse to further refine your search.

As you find new data, enter it into your database, but be sure to mark the source where you found it.

Here, for example, is the notation for one of my databases on RootsWeb:

Laurence Overmire, *The Overmire Ancestry: Descendants of Revolutionary War Veteran, Capt. John George Overmire* (RootsWeb WorldConnect Project, 2016)

Search Tips

1) Try different spellings or the Soundex feature (located to the right of the surname box). Soundex searches for names that sound like the names you enter, so it's a much broader type of search. It is particularly helpful when you don't know how an ancestor spelled his/her first or last name.

2) Type in just the surname and a location to find family members from the same area.

3) Click on the boxes that say "Has Descendants," "Has Notes" or "Has Sources" for the most thorough and well-researched databases. Often, they have informative notes about the individuals in question.

4) Remember that those databases that don't show any sources cannot be considered very reliable. They may be fraught with errors. You might consider them to have important clues, however, which may aid in further research.

STEP TWO: Go to my database *The Ancestry of Overmire Tifft Richardson Bradford Reed* on RootsWeb.com

1. Type the URL rootsweb.com.

2. Under the heading "Family Trees (WorldConnect)," click on the link "World Connect Project Main Page."

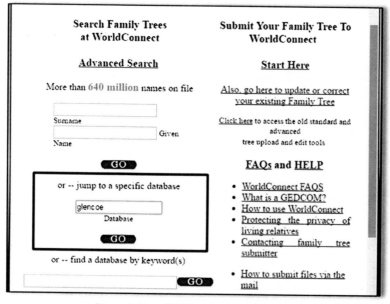

Figure 9 RootsWeb Jump to Database page

3. In the box under "jump to a specific database," type "glencoe" and click "GO."

4. Enter "Overmire, Living" in the search box and click "List."

The Ancestry of Overmire Tifft Richardson Bradford Reed

Entries: 62496 **Updated:** 2016-06-16 03:15:54 UTC (Thu)
Contact: Laurence Overmire, BA, BS, MFA

Home Page: Laurence Overmire's website

Notes on this website are authored by Laurence Overmire unless noted otherwise, and may not be reproduced in any form without prior permission. Updates and corrections with sources appreciated. Please click on any Living individual for important information on how to use this database. [8832609] Visitors since Nov. 23, 2004

Enter surname OR surname, given to find:
overmire, living | List | Advanced Search

No Surname ≤ A B C D E F G H I J K L M N O P Q R S T U V W X Y Z ≥

Figure 10 Search RootsWeb Database for Name

5. Click on any of the "Overmire, Living" entries that appear in the list. This will take you to an Instruction page for how to use the database. Be sure to read it first to help you navigate.

For more than 15 years, I have been compiling this free database as a humanitarian project encompassing over 20,000 hours of genealogical research. The research contained therein is ongoing. The database is meant to be a useful tool to help researchers find their family roots, but it should not be construed as definitive. Some individuals have been researched in much more detail than others. Each individual's page lists the sources for the data. The commentary within the database is my own unless noted otherwise.

Click on any of the links on any individual's page and you can navigate up or down the family tree. You can also view Descendancy, Register, Pedigree and Ahnentafel charts.[13]

When I first began compiling the database many years ago, genealogical research on the Internet was just beginning to take off. Initially, my focus was to identify my paternal grandmother Lillian Tifft Overmire's ancestral tree. Her mother was Lillian Richardson Tifft and her grandmother was Lydia Reed Richardson, who was a descendant of Gov. William Bradford of the Mayflower. As I continued to dig and find more ancestors, the tree grew bigger and bigger and eventually went all the way back to Charlemagne.

I wanted to understand the BIG PICTURE of humanity, to see for myself how we are all interconnected, so I began to trace the ancestries of famous individuals including European monarchs throughout history. It became apparent that the ancestral lines of the British nobility often traced back through the English monarchs into France and Spain and eventually to Charlemagne. As I was tracing I made note of key historical figures – for example, Alfred the Great, Brian Boru of Ireland, Robert the Bruce of Scotland, Lady Godiva, Strongbow de Clare, various English, French, Scottish and Spanish monarchs, etc. And then, as I was tracking their descendants, I

---

[13] Ahnentafel is a German word that means "ancestor table." It lists the known ancestors of an individual including names, dates and places of birth, marriage, and death.

recorded the famous people from whom each individual was descended.

For example, on the page of Alice Morton Bradford, the paternal grandmother of Gov. William Bradford of the Mayflower (my 10th great-grandfather), you will find in the notes that she is a descendant of Charlemagne, Alfred the Great, William the Conqueror, Henry I, Sir William Marshall and Richard "Strongbow" De Clare. She also descends from Malcolm III, David I and the ancient kings of Scotland. Similar notes can be found on the known descendants of ancient royalty throughout the database. By clicking on "Pedigree," it is then possible to trace your way up the tree to find these famous forebears.

A word of WARNING is in order here, however. All of these ancient lines must, of course, be taken advisedly. The further back in time you go, the less reliable the ancestral ties could potentially be. At any point in time there could be an illegitimate child whose true parentage was never made known. Furthermore, we have to rely on ancient pedigrees, genealogies and other records, official or otherwise, whose validity is sometimes difficult to verify. Still, the BIG PICTURE that emerges is certainly indicative of how we are all related.

Today, *The Ancestry of Overmire Tifft Richardson Bradford Reed* contains over 60,000 individuals and, in addition to the European monarchy, traces the ancestries of many famous Americans including Presidents and First Ladies, Founding Fathers, government officials, authors, writers, poets, actors, musicians, artists, scientists, social reformers, religious figures, business leaders, etc. I also investigated many of the immigrants who came to America in the 1600's. Click on an immigrant and the notes will identify famous Americans who descend from each. Click on "Descendancy" and you can see how those lines descend.

The Ancestry of Overmire Tifft Richardson Bradford Reed is a unique resource. You will not find anything else quite like it anywhere. It has received over 1.8 million hits to date and has helped thousands and thousands of people find their family roots and their connections to key figures in history.

It may be of help to you, too. If you click on the Index button at the top of the page and enter your surname, you might find some of your family relations in the database. If so, there could be some useful information of great interest to you and your family. You might even find some ancestral gold!

STEP THREE: Go to FamilySearch

Type in the URL familysearch.org. FamilySearch, historically known as the Genealogical Society of Utah, was founded in 1894. Its primary benefactor is The Church of Jesus Christ of Latter Day Saints (LDS). The site provides free access to many excellent resources including the 1880 census and the U.S. Social Security Death Index. You will need to register and open an account to begin accessing the site. Follow the directions on the screen.

STEP FOUR: Go to Find A Grave

1. Type in the URL findagrave.com. Find A Grave
   identifies individuals whose graves are located
   in cemeteries all over the world. Each
   individual's page is a numbered memorial that
   sometimes includes photographs, notes and
   other pertinent information. You can also pay
   your respects and leave messages and virtual
   flowers. Volunteers even offer to take
   photographs of your ancestors' graves on
   request.

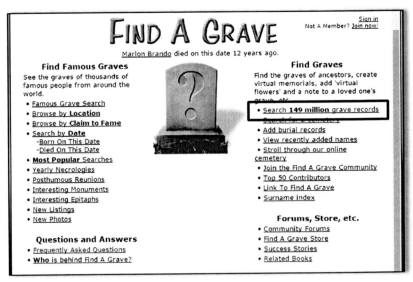

Figure 11 Find A Grave Homepage

2. Under the right hand column marked "Find
   Graves," click on the bullet point at the top that
   says "Search 149 million grave records." This
   will take you to the Find A Grave Search Form.

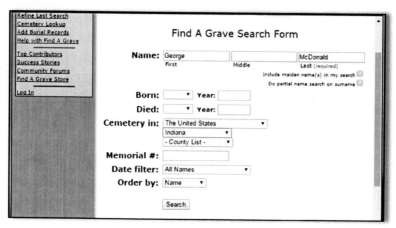

Figure 12 Find A Grave Search Form

3. Type in the first and last name of the individual you are looking for and birth/death dates if known. Sometimes, you will not only find where the person is buried, but his/her family group as well. You might even find some of their ancestors linked generation by generation to the memorials.

4. Check to see if there are any other individuals with the same surname buried in the same cemetery. Often, they will be relatives.

5. To find out more about Find A Grave, go to the link "Help With Find A Grave" at the left margin of the Search Form. If you are one of those people who enjoys walking through old cemeteries, you might even consider becoming a volunteer to help others find their loved ones. It is a tremendous service that they provide.

STEP FIVE: Go to Ancestry.com

1. Type in the URL ancestry.com. This is another valuable resource. As of this writing, they offer a 14-day free trial. Try it out and see how helpful it is for you.

2. If you are serious about pursuing genealogy for any length of time, I recommend paying the annual fee and becoming a member. In my opinion, Ancestry.com is the most valuable genealogical search tool on the market with access to a substantial number of documents and resources including census records.

3. As you are searching on Ancestry, be sure to click on "Family Trees," which are posted by other researchers like yourself. Often, you can find your ancestor in some other researcher's family tree. That person's work may save you a lot of time and effort if they have already done a great deal of research on your branch of the family in question. As always, make sure the information is reliably well-documented.

STEP SIX: Search the Internet for additional clues

Go to Google (or your favorite Internet search engine) and make multiple searches for any relevant information about the individual in question. Often you will turn up little gold nuggets that will help you in your quest.

EXAMPLE SEARCHES

- Type in the first and last name of an individual
- Type in the full name (first, middle and last names)
- Type in full name and spouse
- Type in just the surnames of each spouse
- Type in surname and location where your ancestor lived
- Type in surname and applicable detail of known information, e.g., year died, cemetery where buried, church, historical event (Civil War, etc.)
- Type in various spellings for the names in question

Endless combinations are possible. You never know which combination might strike gold!

Why, just recently I simply typed in the first and last name of one of my client's ancestors and turned up a World War II photograph of that ancestor from 1943 military files. My client was, of course, elated to see it.

It is also advisable to conduct these Internet searches over extended periods of time. As time goes by, new information may become available on the Internet. After many years of struggling to break through impenetrable brick walls, you might suddenly discover documents that were previously unavailable that can lead you to the truth of your elusive lineages.

Following this **6-STEP PLAN** should keep you busy for quite a while.

ADDITIONAL RESOURCES

If you would like to dig even deeper, here is a list of other helpful resources to check out. They can be found by typing in the name or URL in your search engine. Note: some services may require fees.

Access Genealogy (accessgenealogy.com)

AfriGeneas (African American Ancestry, afrigeneas.com)

AncestralFindings.com

Ancestor Hunt (ancestorhunt.com)

Ancestry.com Message Boards

Ancient Faces (ancientfaces.com)

Billion Graves (billiongraves.com)

Castle Garden (immigration records before Ellis Island, castlegarden.org)

Chronicling America (newspapers, chroniclingamerica.loc.gov)

Census Finder (censusfinder.com)

DistantCousin.com

Ellis Island (EllisIsland.org)

Fulton History (newspapers, fultonhistory.com)

Genealogy Resources (refdesk.com)

Genealogy Today (genealogytoday.com)

GenForum (genforum.genealogy.com)

Google News Archive (news.google.com)

Hispanic Genealogy (hispanicgenealogy.com)

Illinois Digital Newspaper Collections
(idnc.library.illinois.edu)

Immigrant Ships Transcribers Guild (immigrantships.net)

JewishGen.org

Library of Congress Online Catalog (catalog.loc.gov)

MyTrees.com

National Archives and Records Administration (NARA)
(archives.gov)

National Archives of Ireland (genealogy.nationalarchives.ie)

National WWII Memorial Washington D.C.
(wwiimemorial.com)

Native Web Genealogy (Native American, nativeweb.org)

New England Historic Genealogical Society (NEHGS)
(AmericanAncestors.org)

Obituaries (Legacy.com)

Olive Tree Genealogy (olivetreegenealogy.com)

Prabook, a source of biographies (prabook.org)

Preserve the Pensions (War of 1812 pension records,
preservethepensions.org)

The Civil War Soldiers and Sailors System (CWSS, nps.gov)

UK National Archives (nationalarchives.gov.uk)

USGenWeb Census Project (us-census.org)

USGenWeb Project (usgenweb.org)

UnitedStatesVitalRecords.com

WorldGenWeb Project (worldgenweb.org)

Of course, this is just a sampling of the wealth of materials available on the Internet that can aid you in your search.

If, for some reason, you are unable to find information on the ancestor you are looking for, then there might not be much information available. At that point, you may have hit the proverbial "brick wall." You might want to consider consulting a professional genealogist.

WHEN TO HIRE A GENEALOGIST

Finding one's ancestry and learning about one's forebears is an incredibly exciting and enlightening experience. I always recommend that everyone do their own genealogy research. Only by engaging in the actual digging yourself will you experience the sheer joy of seeking out and finally uncovering your ancestors.

What you learn in the quest for your own family history will impact your life, the lives of your children, your grandchildren, and the potentially millions of descendants who will follow.

Be that as it may, some people simply don't have the time, the interest, the patience or the energy required to expend on the dig. In such cases, it is a good idea to hire a professional genealogist. A professional with years of experience will be able to work quickly, know where to look, and evaluate and interpret sources and data effectively. His or her expertise could potentially save you a whole lot of time and money.

Understand, however, that the work can be very time-consuming and expensive. The more specific you are as to what you would like to find out, the more likely the genealogist will be able to help you.

A professional genealogist can also provide valuable insights if you are stuck and don't know where or how to continue your search.

NOTES

NOTES

CHAPTER 7

Proving Relationships

As you are conducting your research, you will come across many instances where you need to establish the relationship of one individual to another. Most often that relationship will be a parent-child relationship.

BEYOND A REASONABLE DOUBT

As stated previously, it is always best to establish any relationship "beyond a reasonable doubt." As in any court of law, we will be looking for a preponderance of the evidence that allows us to make sound judgments. Making guesses and assumptions without enough evidence is simply unacceptable. People want to know the truth about their ancestry, at least as much as it is possible to know. When people make guesses and assumptions and share it publicly on the Internet without indicating that the relationships are, in fact, guesses, a great deal of damage can be done and the truth may never be known. Theories are fine, especially in that they might aid further research, but they must be clearly stated as such. In my own work, I decided to flag these questionable relationships with three exclamation points (!!!) and describe in my notes what the issues are (see Figures 5 and 6).

In determining whether or not an individual may be related to someone else, we must accumulate as much evidence as we can and we must ask ourselves not only what evidence supports the relationship but also what evidence disqualifies the relationship.

If you do have a reasonable doubt that one person is related to another, you cannot, in good faith and good conscience, claim that that person is related, no matter how much you might wish it to be so.

TRUTH IS IMPORTANT

Finding the truth, after all, is what genealogy is all about. It is about remembering, honoring and showing respect for those who came before us. Think about it. How would you feel if some descendant of yours in times to come inaccurately reported that you were the child of a completely different set of parents? That you were born in a different year or a different place? That you married someone else?

Truth is important. We shouldn't jump to conclusions when the evidence is lacking. And we must always keep an open mind at all times and be willing to go where the best evidence leads.

The problem for many amateur researchers is not that they are dishonest, but that they don't recognize when they do not have enough evidence to clearly establish a relationship.

EVIDENCE TO PROVE RELATIONSHIPS

Absolute proof is very hard to come by, especially when you consider that illicit affairs and family secrets may prevent us from knowing who the actual father or mother of a child might be. DNA tests might be helpful in that regard.

In essence, what we are looking for is a preponderance of the evidence to clearly establish a relationship to the best of our ability.

The best sources for establishing "proof" include the following:

1. Birth records
2. Death records
3. Church records (birth, baptism, marriage, death, burial)
4. Obituaries
5. Family bibles
6. Gravestones
7. Cemetery records
8. Wills
9. Probate records
10. Census records

Find as many of these sources as possible to clearly establish date and place of birth and death and parentage. You might need to contact local resources in the community in question. Sometimes you can order documents from courthouses, libraries, newspapers, genealogical and historical organizations, etc. Find A Grave volunteers might be able to help by searching for and taking photographs of gravestones.

Often you will find the parents of children clearly identified in one or more of these records. Census records are particularly helpful in establishing family groups and following individuals over the course of their lives. If possible, locate the individual in question over the entire period of their lives. Detailed federal census records are available from 1850-1940. You can often find not only a family group, but a person's occupation, military service and even level of education (1940 census). There are also much less detailed federal censuses from 1790-1840 that show heads of household and the number and approximate ages of others in the household. These can provide important clues about the family in question.

If, after looking for all the records listed above, you are still unable to find someone's parents, then you will need to dig even deeper to try to find more evidence.

Sometimes published books will contain biographies of your ancestors that identify family members. Search for them online by entering the name of your ancestor and the city or county or state in which you know they lived or worked. Birth and death dates can aid in that search as well.

If you still are at a loss and cannot confidently "prove" a relationship beyond a reasonable doubt, you may have hit the dreaded brick wall. Breaking through these brick walls can be very difficult and time-consuming, but the next chapter will give you some tips on how to do so.

CASE STUDY NUMBER ONE

I encountered a case recently where a researcher, let's call him Bob, confidently concluded that an ancestor of his, named Mary McDonald (identified by her daughter's marriage record), was the daughter of Col. George McDonald of the McDonalds of Somerset County, New Jersey. I had been investigating Col. George and his McDonald family for some time. I later wrote a book about them titled, *A Revolutionary American Family: The McDonalds of Somerset County, New Jersey.*

Bob was so confident of his findings that he published it on his website showing the lineage as if it were fact. Yet Bob did not have supporting documents that showed a direct link. He had no birth or death records, no church records, no burial or cemetery records, no family bibles, no wills, nothing that showed that his ancestor Mary McDonald was actually Col. George McDonald's daughter.

Bear in mind also that McDonald is a very common name. The more common the surname, the more careful you have to be, because it is very likely that there will be other perhaps completely unrelated family groups bearing the same surname and living in the same vicinity.

That was the case here. Bob based his conclusions upon the following circumstantial evidence:

1. His ancestor Mary McDonald married a man who had the same surname as an immigrant

who could have been his father and who had
settled in Somerset County, New Jersey.

2. Mary McDonald's descendants were
   Presbyterian as were the McDonalds of
   Somerset County.

3. Mary McDonald was born in New Jersey
   according to census records.

4. Census records also indicated that his ancestor
   Mary McDonald was born about the same time
   as another Mary McDonald, who was known to
   be a daughter of Col. George McDonald, but
   whose eventual fate was unknown.

Remember, we need to prove relationships beyond a
reasonable doubt. Further investigation would cast a
considerable amount of doubt on Bob's theory.

First of all, census records are notorious when it comes
to birth year and place. Often the person who reports to
the census taker gives the wrong information about birth
date and place because they didn't know the correct
information, so they just guessed. The approximate birth
dates of Bob's Mary McDonald ancestor as shown by
census records did not exactly match the known birth date
of Col. George McDonald's daughter. Furthermore, if
Bob's Mary was, in fact, born in New Jersey as the censuses
indicated, we still don't know where in New Jersey.

Secondly, it would not be unusual to find descendants
of Scottish families as Presbyterian, since many of them
were.

Thirdly, a thorough investigation of census records, cemetery and marriage records revealed that there were other unrelated McDonald families in Somerset County in the time period in question, including a Mary McDonald who could not possibly be the same person as Bob's ancestor Mary and may have been the mysterious Mary McDonald who was the daughter of Col. George.

In the end, we are left with a speculative theory lacking enough evidence to make a conclusive determination. It is possible that Bob's ancestor, Mary McDonald, was the daughter of George, but it is equally possible that George's daughter was a different Mary McDonald altogether.

In this case, more research is required to dispel the reasonable doubt.

If you as a researcher find yourself in a similar situation, you can publish your work online in order to help other researchers, but please be sure to make it very clear to anyone who looks at your research that your theory has not been proven and requires more evidence.

CASE STUDY NUMBER TWO

A client whom we'll call Alice was stymied by a brick wall and asked me to help her identify the parents of her immigrant ancestor Mary McCaughey Conner. She had accumulated several good documents including family obituaries, marriage records, death certificates, gravestones and burial records, census data, etc., but none of the documents revealed the identity of Mary's parents.

Obituaries showed that there were some McCaugheys in attendance at the family funerals, but who were they?

To solve the mystery, it was necessary to investigate all the known McCaughey families in the area. Fortunately, McCaughey is a rather uncommon name. Such names make pursuing the genealogy much easier. My search eventually revealed a family group (including parents) that fit the bill. It was the only McCaughey family in the vicinity. Mary McCaughey Conner, as it turned out, had several brothers. Repeated searches revealed that two of these brothers, prominent citizens in their communities, had had their family histories published in both a newspaper and a book. Their father John McCaughey emigrated to America from Paisley, Renfrewshire, Scotland. He had worked as a designer of the famous Paisley shawls. The published stories matched the family tradition that was handed down to Alice by her Conner ancestors.

Furthermore, it was now possible to identify the McCaugheys in attendance at the funerals of Alice's forebears. One was a nephew of Mary McCaughey Conner through one of her brothers.

In this case, the research amassed enough evidence to positively conclude that Mary McCaughey Conner was indeed the daughter of the immigrant John McCaughey of Paisley, Scotland. Though there wasn't a single document that stated that Mary was John's daughter, the circumstantial evidence was definitive beyond a reasonable doubt. The brick wall collapsed!

We'll discuss brick walls more thoroughly in the next chapter. You might think we'd need a stick of dynamite and a sledge hammer. Not so. Genealogical brick walls can only be brought down with determination, patience and a healthy dose of thinking outside the box.

NOTES

NOTES

CHAPTER 8

Blasting Through Brick Walls

It is very frustrating for genealogical researchers to find themselves confronted with a seemingly unsolvable problem known as a "brick wall." Typically, brick walls are those instances where it is impossible to identify a person's parents. The lineage seems tragically lost forever. And in many cases that's true – it is lost forever. Brick walls arise with regularity because of the dearth of documented information and evidence that one is able to uncover. Eventually, every line in your tree ends in a brick wall. Consider yourself very lucky if you can trace any line back to 1700 or before.

Brick walls are particularly troublesome when a person's surname is a very common one. It is made doubly difficult when the first name is common as well. As we saw in the last chapter, Mary McDonald is a very common name. We were unable to find her parents with any degree of certainty. The surname McCaughey, on the other hand, is a much more uncommon name and, consequently, Mary McCaughey Conner's parents were much easier to identify by thoroughly investigating the time and location.

Time and place are always critical in solving brick walls, if they can be solved at all.

Brick walls also require a great deal of patience and usually a good deal of effort over long periods of time to try to solve the puzzle.

THE CASE OF GEORGE MCDONALD

My most exasperating – and liberating – experience with a brick wall came in the case of my wife's 2nd great-grandfather George McDonald (1822-1885) of Parke County, Indiana. I had spent years working on this McDonald family assembling all the critical documents I could find, but there was no birth record for him and nothing that identified his parents. Initially, all I had to go on were census records that showed he was born about 1823 in Indiana.

To give you an idea of how confusing various sources can be, consider the evidence for George: Parke County death records stated that he died at age 63 on Apr. 16, 1885, but his obituary and his gravestone both show he died Apr. 6, 1885. The obituary was published on Apr. 16 and stated that George had died on Apr. 6 and was buried two days later. Cemetery records, meanwhile, showed George died aged 52y, 6m, 8d, but his gravestone recorded his age as 62y, 6m, 8d. The gravestone, in this case, was correct. Calculating accordingly, George's actual birth date was Sept. 28, 1822, not 1823 as indicated by census records.

In order to try to identify George's parents, it was necessary to conduct a thorough search of all McDonalds who were living in the area of Parke County, Indiana, in the early to mid 1800's. This took quite a bit of effort. I thoroughly scoured census records and local histories and entered all the McDonalds I could find into my software program making voluminous notes in order to keep them straight. I developed a number of theories about where these McDonalds might have come from before coming to Indiana – from the Carolinas, Georgia or New York. I had a number of possible leads for George's parents and even two people I suspected might be them, a mysterious J. D. G. McDonald and a Betsey McDonald, but the available information was so scant because of the time period. These were people, after all, who were among Indiana's pioneers. Few records survived from that time.

I finally gave up. I thought I would never solve the mystery and that the lineage and history of these McDonalds would never be known.

Periodically, over the course of several years, as my curiosity was re-awakened, I would revisit my notes and plunk around to see if I could find any more evidence. Again, to no avail.

That is, until one enchanted summer evening, July 15, 2013, when I embarked on yet another search for that enigmatic Mr. J. D. G. McDonald. This time I struck ancestral gold! The initials J. D. G. were so unique, I thought I must be able to find out more about this person somewhere. I did numerous Internet searches and hit upon a Jacob D. G. McDonald in a Union College record in Schenectady, New York. The record showed he was from Somerville in Somerset County, New Jersey.

I knew I had struck the mother lode! That one document punched a hole through the brick wall. I continued a frenzied search that night and many days and nights thereafter turning up more and more evidence, work that encompassed several more months. What I uncovered was so fascinating, so exciting, so historically compelling that I decided I had to write a book about it.

George McDonald (born 1822) of Parke County, Indiana, was indeed the son of Jacob D. G. McDonald, a pioneer doctor who settled in Roseville, Parke County, Indiana, with his wife Betsey Taylor McDonald. Jacob D. G. was the son of Col. George McDonald (mentioned as part of the investigation in the previous chapter), a lawyer who was on the legal team that argued the Indiana Supreme Court case of *Polly v. Lasselle* to abolish slavery in that state in 1820. Col. George was, in turn, the son of Maj. Richard McDonald who served with distinction in the New Jersey militia working with Gen. George Washington in the American Revolution.

There really is no adequate way to describe the elation that one feels in smashing through a brick wall. It is a feeling that will overtake you any time you uncover a piece of ancestral gold. It is a kind of spiritual and emotional awakening, the unlocking of an age-old mystery that can lead you to discover truths about yourself and your family.

Mind you, these McDonalds were not even a part of my own ancestral lineage; they were my wife's family. As a genealogist who has seen the Big Picture of the human family, I get equally excited in tracking down and discovering the mysteries of other people's family trees, because on a very deep, personal level I consider their families, my family. And believe me, after researching and spending so much time with all these McDonalds – George, Dr. Jacob D. G., Col. George, Maj. Richard and the rest – I feel like they are my grandfathers and grandmothers and uncles and aunts and cousins, too. It's a wonderful feeling to so embrace the world.

That's what genealogy does. It opens up parts of yourself that have been closed up, cut off, and disconnected. It will open your mind and open your heart.

Most of us come from dysfunctional families. All human beings have their flaws and all of us have suffered from the thoughtless and careless acts of others. People can be rude and insensitive and cruel, especially in this day and age of social media.

As I always jokingly say, "Dead people are easy to love, it's the living ones who are hard!"

Genealogy can be a very healing experience. Most grandparents have good relationships with their grandchildren: warm, loving and kind relationships. It's the same kind of feeling you get from those who have gone before. We remember the good things about them. We recognize the difficulties of their lives – their challenges, their hardships and their struggles. And we can relate. We can empathize with them. We can love them, unconditionally, no matter what.

TIPS FOR BLASTING THROUGH BRICK WALLS

Here are ten suggestions to help you break through brick walls:

1. Gather all the evidence you can about the individual whose parents you are trying to identify.

2. Examine census records carefully, noting street locations and neighbors living nearby. Neighbors are often related. (George McDonald's mother Betsey Taylor McDonald lived near him.)

3. Gather all the evidence you can about the individual's immediate family, spouse(s) and children as well as in-laws, aunts, uncles, cousins, etc. Sometimes those other relations will have birth and death records, obituaries or published biographies that identify the parents you are seeking or otherwise provide important clues. (For example, I made contact with a 4th cousin once removed, a descendant of the sister of my 2nd great-grandmother, Mary Tobey Overmire. He had a wedding picture of my 2nd great-grandparents in his possession and presented a copy to me.)

4. Identify all the people you can find who share the surname and live in about the same time and place. Organize them in your database and take notes in such a way that you can refer to them easily when necessary.

5. Identify allied families who are associated with the family in question. Often the descendants of these families intermarry over time. Following the descendant lines may yield more clues. Sometimes these families have documents or other materials related to your family.

6. Do repeated Internet searches periodically. Be sure to use variant spellings. Look for published biographies of others with the same surname who may have lived in the same time and place.

7. Travel to the places in question to gather more evidence.

8. Pay attention to given names: first and middle names provide clues to one's heritage. Remember that children are often named after family members or others that the parents knew or admired. Unusual spellings can also be revealing.

9. Try to locate land records to determine where the individual lived and to whom the property was passed.

10. Think outside the box, follow your intuition, be persistent, and never give up.

Pay particular attention to number 7 above. I call it "Lucky Number 7." Sometimes to break through a brick wall the best thing you can do is take a trip to the very place where you know your ancestor lived. Sometimes you can get really lucky and find the answers to many of your questions. Go to the local libraries, courthouses, historical and genealogical organizations and churches. Look for evidence anywhere you can find it. Talk to people. Such trips can be richly rewarding and sometimes it's the only way to obtain the information you need to find your long-lost ancestors.

There is nothing like traveling to illuminate and intensify the genealogical experience, as you will see in the next chapter.

NOTES

CHAPTER 9

The Gold Mine of Travel

Traveling to another place is always an enriching experience, but it is made even more meaningful and intense when you are in touch with your own personal ancestral history. It's like going deep into the heart of the mountain where the richest ore of your ancestral gold mine is waiting to be discovered.

I've done so much genealogical work now that whenever I go to a strange, new place I can usually relate in some interconnected way with the people and the historical venues that I visit. When I hear a surname, for example, in casual conversation, I often recognize that surname as being common to my own family tree. I have grandfathers and grandmothers back in time who shared that surname. It is not unusual that I discover that the people I meet are distant cousins. When I am working for clients, I often discover that they, too, are distant cousins of mine.

NEW DISCOVERIES

The more you know about your ancestry, the more research you do, the more you delve into history, the more fascinating your world will become. Why just the other day I found a document that described my great-great-great-uncle Capt. George Overmire (1842-1896) as being captured at the Battle of Atlanta during the Civil War. My dad, Ray E. Overmire Jr., really enjoyed visiting Civil War battlefields. He had taken my family to Atlanta when I was a boy. We toured the battlefield exhibits at that time, but none of us knew a thing about Capt. George Overmire. We didn't even know he existed. After George was captured, he was sent to the notorious Andersonville Prison. How much more meaningful and resonant would that trip to Atlanta have been if we had known all this?

Let me just give you some more examples from my own experience to inspire you to undertake your own adventures.

PLANNING THE TRIP

As I said before, when researching my wife's McDonald family tree, I discovered her ancestors lived in Parke County, Indiana, and Somerset County, New Jersey. I decided to write a book which later became "A Revolutionary American Family: The McDonalds of Somerset County, New Jersey." I knew I would have to visit New Jersey to see what information I could find on these McDonalds and I wanted to trace the family's origins in Scotland, so we planned a trip to do just that.

We spent weeks just planning the trip. We took long walks to increase our endurance and get our bodies into shape. It was a very healthy and fun time.

Of course, I had done a lot of research ahead of time, so I knew many things that I wanted to investigate. There was reportedly, for example, an old sawmill that the McDonalds had owned and operated near a place called Pluckemin.

Soon after my wife Nancy and I landed in New Jersey, we ventured to Pluckemin and an extraordinary, unforgettable adventure unfolded. We went hunting for the old mill based upon some clues we had. While walking along a river where we suspected it might be, it suddenly appeared ghostlike through the branches of the trees. We met the woman who owned the property. She graciously gave us a tour of the building, which still included the original sawblades and other features. Much of the interior had been newly renovated into a "man cave," an entertainment facility with ping pong, foosball, pool tables and a bar. We had the distinct feeling Nancy's ebullient ancestors would approve!

Figure 13   McDonalds' sawmill, Somerset Co., NJ

AS LUCK WOULD HAVE IT

We proceeded to a local Presbyterian church and, as luck would have it, met the minister who had just driven up to drop off some things. We told him the McDonalds' story. He led to us to a document framed on the wall in the church and, sure enough, there was a chart showing Nancy's ancestor Maj. Richard McDonald and the pew in which he was privileged to sit. The document was dated 1796. That's ancestral gold! Then, he took us to his office where he showed us a map that pictured the location of the McDonalds' house in Pluckemin. He recommended we go to the local library where we would find more church records from the Revolutionary period. We did so and were able to confirm the McDonalds' membership in the church well before the Revolution.

This is the sort of information you cannot find online no matter how much searching you do. You will only find it by visiting the actual place where your ancestors lived.

BEING THERE

There is also something profoundly moving when you meet your ancestors "in person," when you visit their graves, knowing that

Figure 14 Nancy at the grave of Maj. Richard McDonald (1734-1820)

their mortal remains lie just a few feet below you. Nancy and I both experienced such waves of emotion when we found the grave of Maj. Richard McDonald himself.

MAKE APPOINTMENTS

On another day, we had arranged to meet with a local historian and author at the historic Abraham Staats House, a building that once served as the headquarters of George Washington's general Friedrich Wilhelm von Steuben. The historian, as we discovered, was a distant cousin of Nancy's (a relation of Col. George McDonald's wife Sarah De Groot), who still lived in Somerset County. He provided us with even more precious information and insight into the history of the area and the McDonalds in particular. What's more, after I investigated his ancestry a bit, I discovered he was a distant cousin of mine also. We shared an immigrant ancestor in common. Talk about a small world!

TAKE TIME TO EXPLORE

From New Jersey we flew to London and began a completely different adventure on an extended tour of Scotland. We traced the roots of Nancy's McDonald family and I did some investigating of some of the families from my own Scottish heritage. What a momentous experience it was for me to traverse the battlefields at Bannockburn and Culloden, for example, as I remembered my ancestors who fought there. At the little town of Douglas, Scotland, we walked into St. Bride's Kirk, a centuries-old ruin surrounded by a graveyard. Inside, I knelt down and touched the effigy of Sir James "The Black" Douglas, my 21ˢᵗ great-grandfather. In 1329, his good friend Robert the Bruce, while on his deathbed, had asked Douglas to take his heart to the Holy Land to fulfill a vow that he would make a pilgrimage there. The Douglas did so and died there on crusade in 1330 while fighting in battle. His body was then returned to Scotland to lie in his family's burial chapel. The heart of The Bruce was also returned to Scotland and interred in Melrose Abbey.

Figure 15 The author with effigy of Sir James "The Black" Douglas

The Scottish adventure was so extraordinary on so many levels I had to capture it in poetry. That culminated in another book, *The Ghost of Rabbie Burns: An American Poet's Journey Through Scotland*. In the course of putting it together, I contacted some of the people who were instrumental in inspiring Nancy and I along the way including the Duke of Argyll (Chief of Clan Campbell), the renowned historian Ted Cowan and some of our favorite Celtic musicians Isla St. Clair, Steve McDonald (composer of *Sons of Somerled)*, Iain H. Scott (lead singer of the band Scocha), and Steve MacNeil (of the Barra MacNeils), all of whom provided very kind endorsements for the book. None of this would have happened if we hadn't made the trip.

The next summer, Nancy and I made another trip to learn more about her ancestral heritage – this time to Dayton, Ohio, and Parke County, Indiana. We visited cemeteries, libraries, genealogical societies, found a wealth of information and met several local historians. We visited the courthouse in Corydon, Indiana, still standing, where Nancy's 4th great-grandfather Col. George McDonald (1768-1820), a lawyer, argued to abolish slavery before the Indiana Supreme Court in 1820.

Once, while we were eating in an attractive and uniquely decorated western-themed restaurant in a little village called Coxville (formerly Roseville) in Parke County, we struck up a conversation with a man sitting in the next booth. It turns out he was the local historian. He told us the restaurant in which we were eating was originally a general store in the 1820's owned by Moses Robbins, one of the pioneers of the village. I knew from my research that Moses Robbins was the son-in-law of Nancy's 3rd great-grandfather Dr. Jacob D. G. McDonald (son of Col. George). The historian told us Moses's store was eventually torn down and replaced by this restaurant, but the floor beneath us was still made of the original planks from Moses's store! How thrilling for us to know that Dr. Jacob D. G. McDonald and his son, Nancy's 2nd great-grandfather George McDonald (1822-1885), would have walked across these very boards!

These are the kinds of remarkable experiences you can have by visiting the actual places you learn about in your genealogical research. They are life-changing events that you will want to share with those you love.

So you see, the search for your ancestral gold is a never-ending quest. There is always an adventure to be had, whether at your fingertips on the computer or in person by visiting the places your ancestors once lived and loved, worked and died. The mystery of life goes on and on and on...

 Treasure Tip

Plan your itinerary well in advance of your trip.

- Schedule appointments with historians and others you would like to meet. You will probably find that they are happy to get together with you and talk local history.

- Make sure that libraries, museums and courthouses are open on the day of the week you intend to be there.

- Contact cemeteries prior to your visit to facilitate locating your ancestors' gravesites.

NOTES

CHAPTER 10

Sharing Your Work

Of course, the whole point of doing genealogy work is to share it with others. What you find is going to amaze your loved ones. They, in turn, will be able to pass it on to their descendants. What you are creating is a legacy that will endure for years to come.

REPORTS, CHARTS, GEDCOMS

There are many ways to share information. You can do it privately by printing out reports and charts for your family members, for example. You can also share GEDCOMS (GEnealogical Data COMmunications), the standard computer file format that many family researchers use to exchange information. This is all very easy to do. Check your genealogy software for the instructions.

VIDEOGRAPHY

A great way to share family stories is by creating a video. High quality video cameras are becoming so commonplace nowadays, nearly anyone can make a film and either share it privately with family and friends or publicly on YouTube.

Many years ago during a family reunion before my mom and dad passed away, I arranged to interview them on camera. I had them sit on the couch while my brother, sister and I asked them questions about their lives. They told several interesting stories including how they met and fell in love and my Dad recounted how his ship, the aircraft carrier U.S.S. *Bunker Hill* (CV-17), was attacked by kamikazes off Okinawa in World War II. It was a harrowing story of which we knew little. Like many veterans, he had been unwilling in times past to relate his war experiences. We are so glad we took the time to record that interview on camera.

Think of all the people you love. Wouldn't their descendants appreciate knowing their stories and seeing what they looked like, how they talked and behaved? Modern technology gives us the opportunity to record such things as never before. I sure wish I could see video of my great-grandparents or their great-grandparents! All it takes is a little time and effort to create some very special memories. Do it before it's too late. You won't regret it.

PUBLISHING

Eventually, you will probably want to publish your genealogical research in a public way online. You might even choose to write a book. I strongly encourage you to do so as long as you follow standard genealogical procedures for documentation, crediting and sourcing (see Chapter 5). The more people who share their work, the more we can all learn. Other more distant relatives of yours, who perhaps know much less than you, will be able to discover their heritage as well.

Sharing is a very generous act. It's about giving back to the larger community.

ONLINE PUBLISHING

There are many different websites where you can post your work online. One of the most helpful and the most popular is Ancestry.com. People who post their well-documented family trees there provide a great service to others. You can find links to census and marriage records, burial information, family stories, photographs, etc.

Unfortunately, there are many out there who are not particularly serious about genealogy and have a very amateur and careless approach to it all. They post their family trees without doing adequate research and without showing any documentation whatsoever. They copy and paste information from others without crediting or sourcing it. Consequently, the lineages they show can be misleading or even completely false.

There is so much misinformation out there already. We don't want to add to the confusion.

Therefore, if you do decide to post your work online, it is very important to be sure that it is accurate to the best of your knowledge. If you post work that is speculative, you must clearly identify it as such, and it is most helpful if you can explain your reasons for your theories.

The problem with uploading inaccurate information for public view online is that people will quickly begin to share it and spread it all over the place. Once the genie is out of the bottle, it is impossible to put back.

BOOK PUBLISHING

The standards for book publishing are even higher than those for online publishing. If you are going to publish a book of any kind, you should ensure that the material you present is accurate and well documented to the best of your ability. Provide plentiful notes and sourcing so that others in years to come will be able to verify the work.

Publishing genealogy is typically not a moneymaking commercial venture, yet it is extremely valuable and important. Your market will primarily be the living descendants of those you are writing about. If there aren't many living descendants who care about their family history, you probably won't sell many books.

I have published four family histories so far. All of them have been labors of love. I will never be compensated for the considerable amount of time and energy that it took to produce the books, not to mention all the money I spent in travel and expenses while researching.

Printing the book can be very expensive as well. So if you are thinking about publishing a book, research how to do so well in advance. Know what you are getting into and proceed accordingly.

None of the difficulties of publishing, however, have made me regret all the blood, sweat and tears I put into creating the books. They are gifts of the spirit that will be appreciated and cherished for generations by those who wish to know more about their family history.

One of the most memorable experiences of my life came after I published my first genealogy book *One Immigrant's Legacy: The Overmyer Family in America, 1751-2009.* I was asked to be the keynote speaker for the National Overmyer Family Reunion in Rochester, Fulton County, Indiana. Overmyer descendants came from all over the country to celebrate their heritage. It was the first reunion of its kind in over 100 years. None of us who attended and participated in the events of that 3-day weekend, including a BBQ picnic in the barn of an Overmyer family homestead, will ever forget the wonderful time that we shared together.

READY, SET, GO!

After you've traveled down this genealogy road for a while and gained experience in finding your ancestral gold, when you feel ready to publish your work, then by all means do so. Your findings will be of benefit to all. Only by sharing information, documents and sources can we accurately plot the generations over time and be confident of our findings.

Remember, we are always looking for that elusive thing we call truth.

Much of the truth of our ancestry, because it is so far back in time, seems impossible to recover. Fortunately, there is one more tool that can really help us out, a tool that was unavailable to previous generations.

A microscopic bodily substance was discovered in discarded surgical bandages in 1869. In 1943, it was found to be critical in determining our genetic inheritance. Scientists are just now beginning to understand and unravel its mysteries. It may be the key to unlocking some of our most ancient ancestral treasure chests, secrets that have been buried in us all for a long, long time – in our DNA.

NOTES

CHAPTER 11

How DNA Testing Can Help

Absolute proof is very hard to come by in genealogy.

Because there is an opportunity for human error in every step of the record-keeping process and because it is not unusual for people to "make up" stories about their family lineage or jump to conclusions about their ancestry with insufficient evidence, there will always be skeptics, especially among genealogical researchers who demand evidence and may question the lineage from one generation to the next.

Furthermore, there is always the possibility that somewhere along the line going back in time, someone who was believed to be the son or daughter of a certain father or mother may not have, in fact, been that parent's legitimate child. That child may have been adopted or born out of wedlock to an unknown partner. Genealogists call this an NPE (nonparental or nonpaternal event).

The farther you go back in time, therefore, the more questionable the genetic relationships from parents to children become, because there simply is no way of knowing for sure.

That's why DNA testing can be very helpful. It can also be used to "prove" lineages by comparing the DNA test results to paper trails, that is, the research and documentation that identifies the various people in family trees.

DNA tests can be fascinating, but they can also be very expensive and sometimes very confusing. That's the drawback.

There are three types of DNA testing:

1. Y-DNA
2. Mitochondrial DNA
3. Autosomal DNA

If money is not an object, I recommend for genealogical purposes that everyone have their DNA tested – all three tests.

THE Y-DNA TEST

If you can only afford to take one test, the Y-DNA test is the one you should take. It provides the most helpful information for genealogists.

The Y-chromosome is handed down from father to son going all the way back in time, but it is only handed down to males. If you are a female, you will need to have a male relative – brother, father, or uncle – take the test for you.

The Y-DNA test, when complemented by a well-researched paper trail, can establish a person's paternal lineage with the highest degree of certainty possible.

The test is very easy to take. You just get a DNA kit from a testing company and follow their instructions. I did my test through Family Tree DNA (FTDNA, familytreedna.com). All I had to do was swab my cheek, place the swab into the package provided and send it off to the company. There are several different testing companies on the market, so be sure to do some research to determine which company is right for you.

It is also very important to test for at least 67 markers; 111 markers is even better. Anything less than 67 markers will not be very helpful when you are trying to prove genetic lineages.

Once you get the results from the test, and it could take several months, you will need to compare those results with others with the same surname.

 Treasure Tip

The most helpful way for you to understand your Y-DNA test results is to join a family DNA project for your particular surname. They have people who are adept at comparing and interpreting results. For example, there is the Clan Donald USA Genetic Genealogy Project (it's free) for anyone who carries the MacDonald surname or any of its many spelling variations. Check on the Internet to see if there is a group studying your particular surname.

DNA tests are most helpful, as I said before, when you can compare the results to genealogy paper trails. When family researchers compare their notes on different branches of the family, DNA can help establish that one branch is definitely closely related to another. It may even be possible to pinpoint the common ancestor.

Let me give you a few examples. After I had written *A Revolutionary American Family: The McDonalds of Somerset County, New Jersey*, I was contacted by a McDonald descendant who claimed to be descended from my wife's ancestor Maj. Richard McDonald through a previously unverified branch of the tree, but there was no document to prove the lineage. It was all hearsay. I advised him to take a Y-DNA test. He did so and, lo and behold, his results matched the DNA of my wife's brother, a known descendant of Maj. Richard. The lineage was thereby proven to be accurate and because of the paper trail, we knew who the common ancestor was – Maj. Richard McDonald.

I have also come across two cases in which males who had completely different surnames closely matched my own Overmire Y-DNA. These gentlemen had unknown male ancestry a few generations back. They were descendants of some kind of NPE. One of their grandfathers may have been adopted somewhere along the line or born out of wedlock to a man we now know must have been an Overmire (or more commonly spelled, Overmyer). In fact, paper trails did help one of these men to identify his mysterious Overmire ancestor. What an astonishing revelation for him thanks to the DNA.

Unfortunately, at the present time too few people are testing their Y-DNA. The more who test, the more all of us will be able to learn about the various surnames, their lineages and their histories.

So you see, when you or someone in your family takes a Y-DNA test you are doing a favor for all the descendants of that surname. You are adding to the base of knowledge that will help us to link the various branches of the tree together.

MITOCHONDRIAL DNA

Mitochondrial DNA (mtDNA) is passed down from a mother to her children, both male and female. So anyone can test his or her mitochondrial DNA. In effect, this is your matrilineal line of descent from mother to mother to mother all the way back in time.

Comparing your mitochondrial results and paper trails with others who closely match you could provide evidence that you and another person are descended from the same matrilineal line. Practically speaking, however, proving relationships this way is much more difficult to do than with Y-DNA, because most people lack significant paper trails for their maternal ancestors.

The fact that so many of us are unable to compile paper trails of our matrilineal lines is indicative of how our patriarchal culture has traditionally placed so little emphasis on the importance of women and their heritage, regrettably so.

AUTOSOMAL DNA

Autosomal DNA (auDNA) is inherited from the 22 pairs of autosomal chromosomes as opposed to the one pair of sex chromosomes, X and Y. Several companies provide autosomal DNA tests, e.g., 23andMe,[14] AncestryDNA, or Family Tree DNA Family Finder. Each has different features, so it's best to research them thoroughly before making your choice.

Both men and women can take the autosomal DNA test. It can be particularly useful in determining parent/child relationships up to about the 2nd cousin level and it can be very helpful in finding cousins who are related to you, up to about 5th cousins.[15] Again, you will need to compare reliable paper trails to see if you can identify where and how you might be connected to someone.

I have had some exciting successes myself in matching autosomal DNA with some distant cousins. For example, when I compared notes with someone who shared my Buchanan ancestry, I discovered which branch of the Buchanans I almost certainly descend from. In another

---

[14] The 23andMe test also provides information on health and traits.

[15] On FTDNA's FamilyFinder, for example, you can identify and even contact people who are shown to be 1st – 5th cousins. 5th cousins share 4th great-grandparents.

instance I matched my Scott ancestry with a person who traced their Scott line all the way back into Scotland. So now I know my Scott family probably came from Fifeshire in Scotland. That's great to know. I haven't proved it yet, mind you, with documentary evidence, but now I have more of an idea where to look and more of a sense of my Scott family history.

The auDNA test does have its limitations, however. The DNA transmitted from generation to generation diminishes over time. For example, 50% of our DNA is transmitted from each of our parents, about 25% from each of our grandparents, but only about 1.5625% from our 4th great-grandparents.[16] That's only 6 generations back in time. Beyond that level, the DNA transmitted from those older generations can be infinitesimally small. Let's say, for example, that if your paper trail shows Native American ancestry about 9-10 generations back, that Native heritage will probably *not* show up in your DNA report. That doesn't mean, however, that you have no Native American ancestry. It simply means it is no longer detectable in the DNA.

And think about this for a moment: if you do have a Native American ancestor in your tree, that person has a huge tree with billions of ancestors of his or her own. All of them are your ancestors, too. If they don't appear in

---

[16] Roberta Jestes, "Autosomal DNA, Ancient Ancestors, Ethinicity and the Dandelion," DNAeXplained – Genetic Genealogy, dna-explained.com, accessed June 2016.

your DNA does that mean you should disregard them and pretend they never existed? No, that would be very disrespectful to all those grandmothers and grandfathers who played their part in giving you life, wouldn't it?

The auDNA test is also fascinating in that it provides you with percentages of your ethnic background. For example, the test might show your ancestry to be 85% European, 13% Asian and 2% Middle Eastern. However, even DNA experts may have a difficult time explaining to you exactly how these percentages were determined and what it all means. My advice is to take those numbers with a grain of salt.

The truth of our ancient ancestry is global in scope. Our early human ancestors originated in Africa, then about 50,000 years ago began a migration to the Middle East and other parts of the world.[17] Our heritage, then, going back thousands upon thousands of years, spans many different cultures and peoples.

PERSONAL IDENTITY – WHO ARE YOU?

Our personal identity – who we think we are – is important. It shapes the way we live our lives. When you take DNA tests, the results will probably challenge your thinking in one way or another. They may open your mind and your heart. If we consciously understand that

---

[17] Jeremy Thomson, "Humans did come out of Africa, says DNA," *Nature: International weekly journal of science*, Dec 7, 2000, nature.com, accessed June 2016.

we are connected to everyone on the planet, it might even change the way we treat one another.

Again, the main drawback at present with all the DNA tests is that too few people are taking them. As more people take the tests, our knowledge expands and everyone can benefit from the information as we learn how DNA is handed down and affects our lives.

SUMMARY

I encourage at least one male from every family to take a Y-DNA test if at all possible. I also recommend you join a Y-DNA study group for your surname. Otherwise, you may find the results confusing and difficult to interpret.

Those who are really curious will enjoy adding the autosomal and mitochondrial tests. You can have a lot of fun when you find other distant relatives and try to figure out how you are related.

Remember, if you take any of the DNA tests you will be contributing to the body of knowledge that will help us all to understand our genetic heritage going way, way back in time. Think of it as a gift to the world, for that is exactly what it is.

Wouldn't it be great if every surname had a Y-DNA study project? Someday, that may become a reality, but only if a lot more people start taking the tests. If you are really energetic, you might consider starting a study for your particular surname.

The pursuit of one's family history is endlessly fascinating. The quest is made even more remarkable when you comprehend that the DNA we each carry within us has been handed down to us by our mothers and fathers across the eons from humankind's earliest beginnings.

NOTES

CHAPTER 12

Bon Voyage!

Congratulations! With your treasure map in hand, you have now officially embarked on the immortal quest to find your ancestral gold!

The fun is only just beginning.

Now that you've discovered the identity of at least some of your ancestors, you'll want to know more about them. Who exactly were they and how did they live? What challenges did they face? Were they a part of famous historical events?

Again, the Internet is there to aid you in your research. This is the really exciting part of the genealogical journey – discovering your family's ongoing history and seeing how you yourself fit in. Like most people, you might discover things about your ancestors that seem to be a part of who you are today, whether it's how you look, the talents you possess, or the things that you are interested in and are passionate about.

There is a whole new science called "epigenetics" that is just beginning to grasp how much we actually do inherit from our ancestors – more than we ever believed possible.

The stories of YOUR ancestors are already out there – somewhere – waiting to be found.

I've been on my quest for many, many years. It never ceases to amaze me. I continue to find incredible gold nuggets.

Why just a few months ago, I was exploring a branch of my tree that a few years ago was a completely impenetrable brick wall. I discovered to my astonishment that others had posted new research online. I met a 6th great-grandfather for the very first time. His name was Alexander Thomson from Renfrewshire, Scotland. He came to America in 1771 on the ship *Friendship*. Best of all, Alexander left a letter behind that described his reasons for coming to America to begin a new life. That's ancestral gold. That's priceless.

Alexander's story is also a good reminder to the rest of us to be sure to leave our own story behind so that our descendants can know a little bit about us. So while you're documenting your family's past, don't forget to take the time to document the present. Save those family letters and precious heirlooms, preserve the old photographs,

 Treasure Tip

Be sure to date and identify who's who in your photographs. Find the most important ones and make sure your children see them.

and take the time to pass down your own stories to your children, grandchildren, nieces and nephews.

 Treasure Tip

Write your own biography – at least a page or two – and hand it down to your loved ones. Don't worry about the writing. Just put it into your own words. What would you like your descendants to know about you?

Remember, we are ALL a part of the same family tree. Every single person has a fascinating heritage. We are all connected somewhere within those branches climbing all the way back in time.

If you're lucky, you may discover connections to people you know today, people who are your friends and your neighbors. I can't tell you how many times I've heard someone's surname and recognized that they must be a cousin of mine. Several of those distant cousins live within an hour away. Who knew?

When you really get hooked on genealogy, there is no end to the quest. One mystery leads to another. The adventure is never-ending. Isn't that a wonderful way to live your life?

Be sure to take your time and enjoy your journey.

Or, as we say in the genealogy business – Good luck with your research!

NOTES

NOTES

APPENDIX

Understanding Relationships

Ancestor – a person from whom one is directly descended. Aunts, uncles, cousins, great-aunts, etc., are *relations*, not ancestors. For example, if you descend from an uncle of George Washington, you are not descended from George Washington; you are related to him.

Descendant – a person that is descended from a particular ancestor (your grandparents going all the way back in time).

Forebear – another word for an ancestor.

In-laws – relationships through marriage. They are not direct relationships. For example, you are not directly related to your spouse's siblings. They are in-laws.

Nobility – the group of people belonging to the noble (usually wealthy) class in a society or country. Nobles were a hereditary class of aristocrats with high social and political status. Typically, they were descended from royalty. Most of the nobility in modern-day Europe are descended from Charlemagne.

NPE – a non-parental or non-paternal event. These are situations in which a child's genetic parents are unknown, e.g., a child born out of wedlock or an adopted child.

1st Cousin – You and your first cousins have the same two grandparents. Your 1st cousins are the children of your aunts and uncles.

Half 1st Cousin – You and your half first cousins share one grandparent.

2nd Cousin – You and your second cousins share the same great-grandparents, but have different grandparents.

3rd, 4th, 5th Cousins, etc. – Your 3rd cousins share the same great-great-grandparents, 4th cousins share the same great-great-great-grandparents, 5th cousins share the same 4th great-grandparents and so on.

Removed – The word "removed" indicates that two people are from different generations. "Once removed" means that there is a difference of one generation, "twice removed" that there is a difference of two generations and so on. For example, your 1st cousin's child is your 1st cousin once removed; your 1st cousin's grandchild is your 1st cousin twice removed. Another example: your mother's 1st cousin is your 1st cousin once removed, because you are a generation younger. Your grandmother's 1st cousin is your 1st cousin twice removed, since there is a two-generation difference. (Your software program will quickly and easily identify these relationships.)

ACKNOWLEDGEMENTS

When it comes to genealogy, there are so many people that one should thank, because there is an interconnected web of humanity that spans many years all contributing to the process of recording, storing, processing and sharing information: the people who preserve and maintain the records, the people who write down the information in the first place, the people who do look-ups to help you access the archives, the people who spend long hours poring over materials to find the family clues, the researchers who share the data and the details about their own family lines, the historians who track the lineages over time, the authors who write biographies, the librarians who help you find what you are looking for, the designers who build the software programs. I could go on and on and on. So let me just say a big thank you to all those who are involved in this multi-faceted process. Their work is seldom recognized or celebrated, but it is so important.

In my previous books about the Overmire and McDonald families, I worked with dozens of people without whose contributions none of those books would have been possible. I thanked and honored many of them by including stories and short biographies of them in the pages of the books. In this book, it seems appropriate to thank the people who inspired me to get hooked on genealogy in the first place. The reader will be able to relate as you think of your own family and friends who first turned you on to appreciating family history.

For me, first and foremost, that person was my maternal grandfather Irl Fast, who served as the family genealogist and used to take our family on outings to visit the gravesites of our ancestors. There he would tell stories of the past and help us understand what life was like in olden times. He was also one of those in charge of organizing and hosting the annual Fast family reunions. He cared deeply about his heritage and his extended family, many of whom he knew personally, and he passed that respectful awareness, inadvertently it seems, on to me. For you see, I was quite young at the time and not terribly interested in, or appreciative of, the gift he was leaving me.

Secondly, on my father's side, I must single out my aunt Marge Overmire Moulton who diligently kept and maintained the Overmire-Tifft family photos and documents. Like her mother Lillian Tifft Overmire before her, she took it upon herself to see that the various branches of the extended family remained in contact through correspondence.

Thirdly, I am very grateful for the genealogical work of my cousin Dave Moulton, who did a tremendous amount of research in the 1980's on our Overmire tree. It was a small piece of paper he sent with the names of the few known Overmire ancestors that really got me started on trying to solve the mystery of who the Overmire immigrant was.

Fourthly, I must acknowledge my 3rd great-uncle Capt. Axel Hayford Reed (1835-1917). Possessed of an indomitable spirit, Axel was one of the fiercely brave and determined pioneers who helped to shape the tenor of this country and give it the sort of steadfast backbone that would be a hallmark of its character. After leaving the family homestead in Maine and striking out on his own, he made his youthful way to Rochester, New York, engaging in the brickmaking business and working for a time on the Erie Canal, then on to Minnesota where, with the breakout of the Civil War, he enlisted as a private in the 2nd Minnesota Volunteer Infantry. Promoted up the ranks, he was awarded a Medal of Honor for his heroic actions at the battles of Chickamauga and Missionary Ridge in 1863. He lost an arm in the latter fight. But as much as there is to admire about Axel, I am personally indebted to him most for his work as a genealogist and author. Before he died in 1917, he published the *Genealogical Record of The Reads, Reeds, the Bisbees, the Bradfords of the United States of America* (Glencoe, MN, 1915), in which he traced our family's descent from Gov. William Bradford of the *Mayflower*. Axel's book prompted me to investigate and update the Tifft, Richardson, Bradford and Reed branches of the family tree, work that is still ongoing and has led me to become the genealogist that I am today.

Axel's introduction to his book has been an inspiration to me all these years and still urges me onward:

"Our ancestors labored and suffered for us, and for the rich and generous blessings we enjoy. They now rest from their labors; sleeping the eternal sleep, while their posterity 'multiply and replenish the

earth,' dropping by the way-side, one by one, following their ancestry. Is it not right that we, their descendants, should try to make their names IMMORTAL, never dying in our memory, and publish to the world the names of their descendants, their posterity?"

It is with a profound sense of gratitude that I honor Axel's memory here.

Finally, this book, *Digging for Ancestral Gold,* would never have become a reality without the dedicated efforts of my wife Nancy McDonald. She puts up with all of my annoyances and frustrations (especially when it comes to computer issues!), counsels me wisely and keeps me ever on course. She edited, designed and formatted this book turning it into something truly unique and special. I know how very lucky I am to have her as my loving companion in this life.

Again, to all who do the work of genealogy in all of its aspects, my sincere thanks.

ILLUSTRATIONS

ABOUT THE AUTHOR

LAURENCE OVERMIRE is the author of 10 books. He has had a multi-faceted career as genealogist, poet, actor, director, educator and public speaker. As an actor, he appeared on Broadway in *Amadeus* directed by Sir Peter Hall, as well as the television soap operas *All My Children* and *Loving*. He was also executive producer of The Writer's Lab in Hollywood, a non-profit organization to promote quality writing in the entertainment industry.

Overmire's poetry has been widely published in the U.S. and abroad in hundreds of magazines, journals, and anthologies. His most recent offering, *The Ghost of Rabbie Burns: An American Poet's Journey Through Scotland,* is his fourth collection of poems, though it also includes a fair amount of family history and genealogy. It recounts the author's quest to find his ancestral roots and heritage, which according to his great-grandmother Burns' family tradition includes a descent from the uncle of the iconic poet Robert Burns.

Laurence is also the author of five genealogy books, including two epic family histories: *One Immigrant's Legacy: The Overmyer Family in America, 1751-2009* and *A Revolutionary American Family: The McDonalds of Somerset County, New Jersey.* His extensive work on the Overmyers and the McDonalds of Somerset County, arguably

Laurence Overmire

the oldest branch of the McDonalds in America, has made him the world's leading authority on those ancestral lines of research.

To help others become aware of their intriguing ancestral ties, Overmire researched many of the early immigrants to America, tracing not only their celebrated ancestors, but also the prominent Americans who descended from them. He published this work in several genealogical studies online, most notably on RootsWeb in *The Ancestry of Overmire, Tifft, Richardson, Bradford, Reed*, which has received over 1.8 million hits and includes the family trees of many U. S. Presidents and European monarchs, and a host of famous statesmen, soldiers, artists, actors, writers, poets, musicians, scientists, inventors, and social reformers. As one of the pioneers in this type of research online, he has helped hundreds of thousands of people discover their family roots and find their intimate connections to the people and events that have shaped world history.

The book that has drawn the most worldwide attention, however, is a philosophical work titled, *The One Idea That Saves The World: A Call to Conscience and A Call to Action*. Overmire calls it "a blueprint for world peace." It has been widely acclaimed for its compassionate, common sense approach to many of the world's most pressing issues.

Laurence is a member of the Sons of the American Revolution (SAR). He graduated *summa cum laude* from Muskingum University, B.A., B.S., and the University of Minnesota, M.F.A., and now resides in West Linn, Oregon, with his wife Nancy McDonald.

For more about the author, go to: LaurenceOvermire.com
For bookings, please contact nancy@imarkbooks.com

Lightning Source UK Ltd.
Milton Keynes UK
UKOW02f2339200916

283473UK00001B/137/P